Endorsements for Jacky's work

D1425889

Be an Angel—
CLEAR THAT CLUTTER!

Fun ideas to organize your home

Jacky Newcomb

FINDHORN PRESS

Published in 2014 by Findhorn Press, Scotland

ISBN 978-1-84409-637-4

Edited by Jacqui Lewis
Cover design by Richard Crookes
Interior design by Damian Keenan
Printed and bound in the EU

Published by
Findhorn Press
117-121 High Street,
Forres IV36 1AB,
Scotland, UK

t +44 (0)1309 690582
f +44 (0)131 777 2711
e info@findhornpress.com
www.findhornpress.com

Dedication

To my husband, John Newcomb,
my clutter-clearing angel
and the inspiration for this book
who did everything except write it.

Contents

If it's stashed, it's trash!

In the consumer age we have access to pretty well anything we want. Assuming you can afford to do so, if you need or just crave an item, with three clicks of your computer mouse the item is ordered and, within just a few days – or sometimes less than twenty-four hours – the object is in your possession.

I wonder if anyone ever sat down and thought about what might happen if we continued to buy items and never let anything go? Years ago, furniture used to be passed on from one generation to the next because, for most people, household items would have been made personally for them or bought after much saving had taken place. Items were cherished and cared for. Things were carefully stored after use and anything that was damaged would be mended rather than thrown away. Socks were darned; fuses were changed; moving parts were oiled.

These days when something doesn't work we often don't even attempt to repair it; we just go out and buy a new one: new clothes, new electrical goods and all the latest gadgets. The old items are chucked in a drawer; hung in the back of the closet; tossed in the spare room; passed up into the attic or stashed in the garage. If you're lucky enough to have a basement or a garden shed, unused items may well be stashed here too. For many people, once they run out of room at home the obvious answer appears to be to hire a storage unit and stash items there too! Does it ever occur to us to just get rid of unwanted items?

I know that each time my family had a new computer the old one ended up in the attic; and now I wonder ... if the current one had broken down, would we have climbed up and retrieved the old one and brought it back into circulation? No! Of course not! At one point we had three fish tanks stacked in the rafters; old rugs, curtains (which we had never used); old pictures we never hung up again;

stacks of old china that we'd replaced and boxes and boxes of old toys that were never brought down and played with again! The horrid truth, dear reader, is that "if it's stashed it's trash!"

So what is clutter?

Clutter is basically anything you no longer want, need or love. Any given pile of items that has gathered mysteriously in the corner of the room, cupboard, closet, garage … you get the idea. Clutter is the boxes of unsorted photos; piles of old craft items for a craft you no longer do; and stashes of old hobby items you haven't touched and opened in several years. Worse still, clutter can be old letters – sometimes unopened – empty boxes and unused gifts. It's also things you don't like: things people have "gifted" you and mementos from occasions you no longer recall. Clutter is belongings that represent the person you used to be or items that remind you of things – and people – that you'd rather forget! If it makes your heart sink to look at it, then it's time to move it on. It's time to remove the energy-zapping "things" out of your life for ever!

How did this book come about?

Having been "lucky" enough to have inherited a lot of belongings in the past, I understand the word clutter all too well. A lot of my own clutter sort of snuck its way into my life without me even noticing it had arrived. I've also always been a bit of a collector and never bought one item in isolation in my life! If I needed something I always bought a spare and usually two spares. I've also had numerous hobbies over the years; crochet, cross-stitch, reading, painting, patchwork … I could go on and on (my husband John says I do!) Each time I took up a new hobby I had to buy everything that hobby required; I needed the whole kit and I needed it now! Surprisingly, perhaps, I did at least buy storage for all of it too!

The trouble with hobbies is that once the excitement of the activity wears off and we become bored with it, we almost never go back to it. The products of who we were then and what we did while we had that hobby just get added to the pile. That pile just gets bigger and bigger and there comes a point when it's time to stop. We have to turn round and address ourselves sternly and say, "Time to clear up your clutter!" (You can say it in a kind voice if you like, but the cross voice tends to work better for me.)

I've actually cleared my stuff in a big way several times. After thirty years I've got pretty good at it. I have become fascinated by the way in which both clutter, and the lack of it, affect your life. Clutter drains your energy, whilst organized and open space completely energizes you. Don't get me wrong, I'm not a minimalist – I have great piles of costume jewellery! And I still have a few collections around, but these are mainly lifelong loves. Over time you begin to learn which of your belongings are "marriage material" and which ones are "one-night stands"! The items that really have meaning to me are now stored beautifully, often arranged and displayed so that as well as loving owning and using the items I can enjoy their appearance, colours and shapes.

I've written a few articles about clutter-clearing and I even have a Facebook page about the subject. I have a few things to say; I've learned a lot about the art (and there aren't many people who are born with the skill and don't have to learn), and I've picked up a few tips along the way. If you're drowning in clutter, as I've been in the past, why not join me on a journey of discovery? I'm hoping you'll be inspired by my stories (and the ideas from other people, dotted throughout the book) to set to and begin clearing and organizing your own home.

Take my advice: if you're reading and feel inspired by anything at all, put down the book, jump right up and set to work immediately. Each beautifully organized home starts with a tidy sewing box or the bathroom cabinet. One step at a time!

You can barely switch on the TV these days without seeing a show about hoarding; the latest "makeover show". Oh how we love to judge those people whose rooms are piled to the ceiling with old newspapers; "useful" broken items waiting to be mended and old packaging of every sort. How on earth could someone get into that state, we mutter. Easy: it begins with just one newspaper.

Real hoarding is often the result of inner turmoil following a trauma or loss and the most severe cases require much support and assistance from counsellors, doctors and other professionals to get to the root of the problem before the person is able to get rid of the "stuff" in their life.

Serious hoarding is an illness, like alcoholism or drug-taking. "Stuff" is a protection against the world; it's a way of trying to hang on to what has been lost; "padding" to prevent the hurt reaching in. If you know someone whose habits have reached this point, or you feel that you yourself are in this situation, then do seek professional help. Don't try to do this alone, it's just too overwhelming. A book can only go so far and no one person can step into your shoes. Clutter is the thin end of the wedge – hoarding is always a potential destination; I know, I could easily see how that next step might happen.

As you'll discover from my own clutter-clearing journey, I had my own reasons for gathering things around me. Maybe you'll recognize some of your habits as you read about mine, or perhaps you'll laugh out loud at your own collecting patterns. The reasons we gather "stuff" around us are many and varied. Who's to say what is "clutter" and what is a much-loved collection?

Clutter is the word I use for when the belongings around you prevent you from living a productive life. If you have to step over a pile of clothes to reach the bathroom you may be in trouble. Do you have to wade through the children's toys every day just to switch on the TV? Is your kitchen full of items just waiting to be recycled? One of my sisters used to be nicknamed the "bag lady". She always had a hall full of clothes waiting to go to the charity shop or for her to sell at the second-hand store; and yes, they were gathered in plastic bags. Yet, as is the case with many of us, these items rarely made it out of the door. Maybe you spend several minutes each day searching for your keys or looking for your handbag? Getting organized can save you so much time as well as give you breathing space!

My own home used to be full of unfinished items. I owned a half-made cushion that I'd been quilting for fifteen years. I only knew this because I had moved house twice and it still hadn't been finished. Faced with the prospect of throwing it away I vowed to complete the project before our latest move. I had just ten days to go. I reached my deadline but after so many years the cushion was now only fit for the cat basket; it was no longer fashionable! Sometimes *time* really is of the essence! More on this later....

Although my clutter was fairly organized and clean, it had become a dangerous habit. I admit I had replaced lost items only to rediscover them at a later date, buried under something else. I had bizarre collections and had overbought on certain things. I also had an attic and a garage full of objects I was saving for some unknown date in the future – or worse, saving it for someone else who would probably not want it anyway. Does any of this sound familiar?

In these times of plenty it's easy to accumulate objects at an alarming rate. With the ease of internet shopping we don't even have to leave our houses to buy things. Even the language is exciting – we "win" an object we've bought in an online auction; no wonder we buy so much. Is life really a competition, where the "winner" is the person with the most stuff at the end of their life? The biggest problem is that we continue to buy and forget to remove possessions from our ownership. If you continue to pour water into a glass, it doesn't take a genius to know that eventually the glass will overflow. This is what we have done to our houses; too much coming in and not enough going out.

Are you a hoarder? Maybe not to such extremes, but could your home do with a little light editing? I bet it could! There isn't a person I know who couldn't manage with a little less than they have right now (including me).

Is clutter normal? No, but it's certainly usual. Overbuying has become a national pastime but it doesn't have to stay that way. The behaviour we have learned can be unlearned. I'm not advocating a minimalistic lifestyle (actually that's not MY style either); but everyone can benefit from control, right? Really, I promise – less is more.

There is no such word as "should" in this book. After all, your belongings are yours to do with as you wish. What I think you'll find as you read along, though, is that clutter is hidden everywhere in our homes. Sometimes we just stop noticing that it's there. I want you to notice your clutter and see if some of it can be lifted (notice that word "lifted") out of your home. As each bag or box of unwanted items leaves your home you'll feel lighter and you'll feel personally more "lifted" too.

At first it's really difficult to let anything go – I struggled over silly little things – but eventually you'll find yourself throwing and giving away possessions with complete glee! One might even say you feel a "high" from it that is every bit as exciting as buying stuff. I've found that I actually love clearing things from my home now; it gives me more space, sometimes just space to change things round a little and freshen up. Now when I want something new I say to myself, "What can I sell to make money to buy this with?" At the very least I am always aware that I need to give something away to make room for the something new. I'm trying to live with a "One In, One Out" rule. I am at peace with the more spacious home I live in. I like that there are a few gaps on the walls and shelves. It's a new comfortable place for me. Even the kitchen cupboards have room to breathe.

First the rubbish leaves the house, then the duplicates. Next the damaged or broken things, followed swiftly by the objects you no longer use. Hardest of all are the objects that cost a lot of money but are sitting in a cupboard still unwrapped, or in their boxes. Does it really matter how much they cost, though, if you never use them? What about those items you inherited or were given as gifts by people you love? But don't panic; it's possible to get shot of those too – and you'll even feel good about doing it!

This is my personal journey; I lived it and so did my family! I wasn't buried in stuff (well, apart from the ironing cupboard) but I did have too much. My stuff for the most part was well organized, but don't be fooled, even "filed" stuff is still just organized clutter. Heck, sometimes even the storage is clutter (don't get me started on the broken plastic boxes in ugly colours!). Yes, I let it all go and treated myself to new storage once I had cleared out the things I no longer wanted. You can do this too!

So come with me on my clutter-clearing journey. I've read all the books, I've watched all the shows and now I am wearing the T-shirt! I've literally walked the walk (several times) and now I am talking the talk. I'm hoping that some of the chapters will inspire you so much that you put down the book and immediately start sorting something! Go for it … and of course, let me know how you get on!

CHAPTER 1

How I got in this mess in the first place

*"Don't own so much clutter that you will be
relieved to see your house catch fire."*
— ***WENDELL BERRY,*** FARMING: A HANDBOOK

One day we were the owners of a small semi-detached house and the next we had inherited a half-share of the home belonging to my late father-in-law. His sudden passing left us deeply shocked, and still grieving we travelled the two hours to his home. Sitting in his bungalow I looked around at a lifetime of belongings and summed up the situation. We needed to move our share of his belongings out of the house as quickly as possible and sell the house.

As we were not local I could feel a sort of panic inside of me. Many of his belongings were expensive, and in a way that made the problem even more difficult to deal with. When you've lost someone you love, the idea of getting rid of their things almost feels like you are giving away the only link you have left to that loved one. Parting with a deceased person's objects is like giving *them* away too. It fills you with guilt. Logically we know it's only someone else's stuff, but stuff like that becomes attached to your life like Velcro; those hooks are really hard to shake off! The fact that so many of his objects had real monetary value only made the whole thing worse – after all, we couldn't exactly put it all in boxes and take it along to the local refuse tip, now could we? We could have, of course, but at the time it never even entered our heads.

We piled up the car and drove load after load home: books, china, cut glass and pictures. Moving the large furniture meant hiring a van. Many of my father-in-law's possessions were quality objects, signs of an affluent lifestyle. Maybe I wanted a piece of the lifestyle, but the problem was that his belongings were treasured by and held special memories for someone else, not us. My husband John, who isn't generally attached to much, seemed to struggle with emotional attachments to some of his parents' possessions. He delayed making decisions by hiding smaller items in his desk, then a box, then the attic – keeping "inheritance clutter" is obviously catching even for those who don't normally get caught up in hoarding! Among the objects were ship paintings and framed etchings. The etchings were clearly antique, so although they were not my taste at all we still hung them up all around our own home.

The house wasn't nearly big enough, so we paid out a large part of our inheritance to make room for the new objects: we literally extended our house! When I look back it all seems so silly – why would you make your house bigger to house someone else's stuff? I wish I'd been an outsider looking in to see how ridiculous the whole exercise was.

We actually lived that way for around twelve years. After redundancies and various other financial issues around trying to run a very big house, we decided it was time to move to somewhere smaller and more manageable. Someone kindly lent me a book called *Clear Your Clutter with Feng Shui* by Karen Kingston. It's a small book and I read it cover to cover. Boy, did it have an immediate effect! As I started to read through Karen's stories from clients and how their lives had changed for the better as a result of getting rid of "stuff" from their lives, so I was encouraged to do the same in our house. I began working like a woman possessed and right away began organizing, sorting and most importantly throwing things away. It was brilliant! I went out and bought my own copy of the book. I've reread it four times over the years and each time it's spurred me into action again! There is something rather exciting and inspiring about reading other people's clutter-clearing stories; it helps you to relate and begin to notice similar patterns and actions in your own house and your own life. I'd still recommend this book now.

Taking things to the car boot sale

Because we wanted to move to a much smaller house (half the square footage) we had a lot of items to remove, so I wanted to be ruthless. The reality was a little different though. I did get rid of loads of items but it was much harder to do than I had ever imagined. At first the family and I gathered up carloads of items and took them to a local car boot sale. We did this for six weeks and the final week we sold whatever was left on our table to another stallholder for a fixed price. I was not bringing that stuff home!

The first week we managed to make a healthy sum of money. Our haul had included things such as a brass fireguard and I clearly remember feeling angry that someone offered us so little for it, but where we were going we didn't need it. Boot sales and yard sales are not the best way to make a LOT of money but they can be a way of selling a lot of items quickly – as long as you are ready to let things go at rock-bottom prices.

The kids got bored; there are so many other stalls with what start to look like tempting items for sale; it is easy to just pick up a burger from the burger van (even if you have packed sandwiches and a flask to help economize). Your own food rations don't last long when there are only a few people walking round and even fewer buying, it's raining and you are blocked in by other cars.

Don't let me put you off though – this is a way of generating some income from your items and, for many of us, generating extra income is one of the goals.

READER'S EXPERIENCE
My clutter is in the loft; the house will be coming down round us if any more goes up there! We should do a boot sale really...
— *MELDA*

House sale

In England not many people sell things right from their front yard but because our house was on a main road we decided to give it a go. Full of optimism, we priced everything and took it outside. Almost right away it began raining and, looking out from inside the house, I was ready to cry; I also felt embarrassed about the whole thing – what if no one came? Would people laugh at us?

We sat watching the rain run down the windows for a while, but about an hour later it all dried up. The posters we had earlier put up outside had attracted some attention and we did have one or two callers come right into the house and buy things. Whether it was embarrassment or what I'm not sure but I could hear words coming out of my mouth like, "Oh you can have the tablecloth free with the table" and "If you like the lamp you can have both of them as they come as a set … ."

Again, we did OK with this method but I realize I could have been a better salesperson! If you sell from your house make sure you are a little tougher than I was, or at least stick to the prices you've given things, work out in advance any "two-for-one" type deals you'd like to offer and don't change them.

Postcards in shops

We created postcards with images cut from magazines of similar items to those we were selling and put them up in shop windows in our village. At the time we didn't have a camera attached to a computer so this was the best way! Larger pieces of furniture sold well like this and because people knew the price in advance we sold the items more or less for what we had originally asked for them. Success! I even remember doing pencil drawings of items when we couldn't find a picture. It worked just the same.

Charity

After a month and a half we still had piles of things left and the house move was imminent. A friend suggested that a local women's refuge centre were always looking for household items so that women who'd escaped abusive relationships could set up new homes. This was music to my ears. We cleared out a whole room and that gave us somewhere to put the other stuff that was waiting for a new home. It's amazing how much easier it is to get rid of things if you know they are going to a better home. This is a useful tip to remember. Among this stuff were some things I had wanted to keep, but space in our new home was an issue so I had to let the excess go. Would knowing that your stuff was going to a good home like this help you to let things go?

READER'S EXPERIENCE
I had a lot of "organized" clutter but just after Christmas I de-cluttered and sent it to charity shops. Now I'm trying to be more organized and not to buy things I don't need!
— *LAURA*

There is reluctance in many of us to take things to landfill, and with good reason. Who wants to have their old objects buried underground, messing up the earth for future generations? There is something rather obscene about throwing things away when they can be recycled, right? Objects that were borderline in my mind (shall I keep or throw this?) were decided each time I asked the question, "Would someone be really grateful for this?" The shelter said that they took almost everything including toys. Our eventual haul included:

- A sofa and armchair
- A coffee table
- A computer and computer table
- A television
- Pictures, photo frames
- Lamps
- Rugs
- Curtains and cushions
- Sheets, bedding
- Cookware
- Utensils (there were plenty of duplicates from our inherited house – three potato-mashers, for example!)
- Cutlery and crockery
- Clothes, children's clothes and shoes
- Toys

We filled our second sitting room right up to the ceiling and the shelter arrived with a large van to take the stuff away. I slept well that night, knowing that several women would benefit from our goodies; giving to a good cause really helps the transition process along.

"Transition process": moving from being a person who accepts clutter as a part of their life to one who doesn't!

If you have large quantities of things that you need to clear quickly, do consider this method; knowing that you're helping others is one of the most satisfying ways I've experienced of getting rid of stuff.

"Magnetic" items

When you're a hoarder you find that similar items seem to collect together. Being a spiritual person, much of my personal clutter was a spiritual type of clutter. I was stunned to discover that I had incense sticks in several different rooms; likewise bottles of every type of aromatherapy oil; boxes of candles; and piles and piles of self-help books just hidden everywhere.

One of my biggest hoards has always been books. As well as reading books, of course I write them too. I've written piles of books on real-life stories of guardian angels and miracle-type experiences, so of course the house was full of angel-decorated objects too.

When I was growing up I was one of three sisters (another sister was adopted into the family much later). When money was short I remember Mum buying one packet of sweets and sharing it between the three of us. There were other shortages too; I could never find a matching pair of socks to wear to school. There just never seemed to be enough to go round.

I recall all the neighbouring kids coming to play at our house; and half the village always seemed to be at ours for tea. We still had more than most people we knew, but I always felt moments away from panic about the possibility of not having enough or having to share it.

No doubt you have your own story, but once I started to earn money of my own I began overbuying everything, compensating and overcompensating for the small areas of my own youth in which we didn't have enough. I think I just never wanted to have to share things ever again.

Years later, when my own kids were young, I would buy stacks of pairs of matching socks for them so they always had plenty of socks for school. They had enough money to buy whatever sweets they wanted (and were happy to share with anyone!).

Your own clutter will always have a story behind it somewhere. You might know what your stories are, or not. As I discover each new habit of mine it makes me laugh, but for some people it might make them cry. We hoard because of trauma or loss, usually; the bigger your clutter pile the bigger your issues! It's true! (No judgements here.)

Velcro objects

So back to the Velcro objects I talked about in the introduction. Not real Velcro – the fastening tape made of "hooks and loops" – but the "stickiness" of objects you can't shake off. Among those items we keep because we feel guilty are inherited objects. Great Aunty Rosie's tea-cups, mother-in-law's teapot, father-in-law's ship pictures … I could go on. I know you'll have items just like these in your own home! We'll explore this phenomenon more as we go through the book.

Sometimes I used to put stuff in a box to go to the charity shop and a few days later would find myself taking it back out again…. When John realized this was happening he found a way to fix it. He would empty the box into another in the back of the car to stop me seeing it. I would think it had already gone to the charity shop and would never worry about it again. He'd realized that the boxes had to be taken out of sight quickly to stop me changing my mind. Hiding them from me and letting me assume they'd left the house already worked. He was a sneaky helper and I only discovered this secret very recently! Thank you, dear husband.

READER'S EXPERIENCE
I'm afraid that I confess to having rather a lot because a lot has been gifted to me; it's full of sentimental value. And there

are the bits that belonged to "so and so" and must always be treasured because so and so has now moved "upstairs".

— *CORRINA*

The Chinese jug

When I was ten years old, my sisters and I were given a small sum of money from our parents; we headed off to a local antique shop under Mum's guidance. Mum wanted us to buy something "to last", a treasured object we might keep for our future homes. It sounded like a wonderful idea and it was intended as a life lesson. Three little girls happily wandered around the shop but I soon realized I had precious little money to buy any of the things that I actually wanted. After we'd walked round and round Mum was getting impatient; my two sisters had chosen something for themselves but I was panicking now; I couldn't find anything I liked and to be honest, I would much rather have spent the money on sweets or a book.

Just when I was about to give up I noticed a small patterned jug. Even my untrained eye could tell that it was Chinese. I checked out the price tag and breathed a sigh of relief; I could afford to buy it! I handed over my money to the shopkeeper. I didn't love the jug – if I am honest, I didn't even like it that much – but knowing I was buying it for the future, I was happy to go home and put it into the attic.

Many years later I was sorting through some objects to give to the charity shop when I spotted the jug. I picked it up and really examined it. An important thing to remember about objects in your house is that they have to either serve a purpose or be something that you enjoy having around and looking at. Did I like it? No! Was it useful? Not really! Did it fit into my décor? No! Right, I decided, I was an adult and it was time to throw it away. I added it to the pile of objects waiting to be donated but right at the last minute I retrieved it from the pile. It had Velcro on it – invisible hooks of guilt that meant I was unable to let it go. I remembered the day I'd bought it. It was precious; something for my future ... wasn't it? I'm ashamed to say the jug came right back in off the pile and was put back in its place on the shelf in my living room. Damn!

Now, even more years later, I was ready to get rid of it again. As I sorted through the items for the women's refuge the jug went into the room along with everything else to be collected. Moments before the van arrived I walked back into the room and spotted the jug on the table. I couldn't help it. I picked it up and took it back, this time hiding it in the cupboard!

Moving house

Eventually we moved to a smaller house. We still had a lot of stuff, so boxes of items went up into the attic – not just a few things but a lot of things. My brain was done. I was exhausted and unable to get rid of another thing. Part of me was keeping things because I believed that one day I would live in a larger home again and I was keeping things for that day. At least I had got rid of many things I didn't like; that was a very big start! I forgave myself. Nobody's perfect ...

READER'S EXPERIENCE

Anytime I de-clutter I end up putting it up in the attic. Now I need to spend a week up in the attic to de-clutter it!

— *DIANNE*

The attic

If we'd ever had a house fire, we'd have been in serious trouble. At one point we had mice wandering around the coving and then years later we had a wasps' nest in the attic. It would get so hot up there that dead wasps would drop down through the edges of the attic door. I remember going up with some special spray to try to kill them off. The buzzing went quiet for a few days but then started up again. There were so many boxes up in the attic that it seemed easier to ignore them than work our way around them to clear the nest.

Many weeks later the buzzing was so loud that we had to venture up the ladder to take a peek. We were stunned; the nest was now the size of an armchair and it was time to stop denying the problem. We had to call in a man from the local council to deal with it. He was shocked and said it was the second biggest nest he had ever seen; at that point I felt ashamed!

He smoked the nest, did some other technical stuff and then left. "Aren't you going to take the nest away?" I asked naively! He smiled and said, "No, leave it around ten days and then they should all be dead, then you can break it down and remove it."

Wasps are sneaky buggers and know how to build to last. The nest wove its way around the attic beams and even under the roof felt. The texture of a wasps' nest is a little like papier mâché and is really strong. We threw away things that they had built onto (it's one way of clearing your clutter!). I had to pay my sister to come and help me remove it (she'd probably have done it for free but I felt so bad asking for her help that I insisted she take a fee). We had to use a large bread knife, dustpan and brush and vacuum cleaner as well as large dustbin bags. We managed to remove the nest but we still hadn't cleared the attic!

READER'S EXPERIENCE

I hate clutter. I pass baby clothes on to friends and family so they can be reused, but most of the baby stuff is in the loft. It's hard to sell baby stuff on.

— *TRACY*

CHAPTER 2

A clutter-clearing journey

Clutter-clearing is a journey not a destination

The dining table

In the past, I'm afraid I used to be very sneaky with some of the bigger objects I wanted to keep but could no longer store. I persuaded my own parents to buy the dining-room table I'd inherited, as well as the matching mahogany and glass corner cabinets. I figured that one day they would be ready to get rid of them and we'd be able to buy them back or inherit them for a second time.

Mum and Dad took care of the dining table in particular; and although it was used every week when the family came over, it was always covered with a felt pad and layers of tablecloths. When Mum and Dad decided to move to a small apartment we had to make a decision about the furniture. We were still living in the small house and still had nowhere to keep the table, so we did take it back and we put it into storage. Can you see what's coming next?

Months later, when we were still not in a position to move to a bigger house, we realized we'd have to sell the furniture after all. My husband took a day off work and we rented a van to clear the whole lot and take it to the local auctions. We drove over and parked up and carefully lifted the tabletop out of the back of the van; there were no protective covers laid over the top this time and another piece of furniture was balanced alongside it. All of a sudden both pieces of furniture slipped down, leaving a large scratch on the tabletop! After all these years of careful handling it was ruined. I was completely shocked and for a moment was ready to cry, but instead I burst out laughing at the complete ridiculousness of the whole thing.

The furniture had cost me hundreds of pounds in storage (about £600), plus a day off work and the hiring of a van to take it to auction. All that and I'd never even used it. Guess what? After selling all the furniture we didn't even make our money back from the hire of the van! Finally, as I stood there laughing, I felt that I'd let the furniture go.

Lesson? Never store items "just in case"! I would NEVER again put anything in storage ever again. Most people who put things in storage don't even recall what they have stored there. If you can't fit it in your house then you don't need it. No one can afford to waste money each month on a "mini-house". And never ever store things just in case someone else will want them one day – they won't!

Throw, sell or donate!

When we moved to our present home (a big house again) we had a rule; nothing goes in the attic. Even the Christmas trees (yes, we had two) found a home inside a built-in cupboard. In the end just two extra-large empty suitcases made their way to the attic and we flattened down and stored a few boxes from the move for when we moved again. That's it. Apart from those few things, the attic is clear!

We've now moved house again. Originally my husband and I had found a new home by the sea, but we were four and a half hours' drive from our family and friends, so now we're back. We started clutter-clearing in earnest before we left. Only items we chose to display or use – in other words, those things we loved and needed – got to stay. Everything else had to earn its place in our home. Guess what? I gave away one of the Christmas trees!

READER'S EXPERIENCE

I am currently in the process of packing boxes because we move in three weeks' time. I have taken this opportunity to have a really good sort-out. It feels very cleansing. A lot of stuff has gone to family/friends and the charity shop. We're only taking what we actually need. There is no room for clutter anymore in our lives.

— *CATHY*

Some reasons why we clutter-clear

Usually we need an incentive to get started on the junk pile, and sometimes it's easier if there is an urgent need:

- A house move
- Visitors coming to stay
- A death in the family
- A new family member due
- Damage from fire, flood etc.
- Space needed to run a business or do hobbies.

Hopefully, though, you'll be clutter-clearing just because you know it's time! Don't wait for the urgent need. I always worried about what would happen to the mess if something happened to me. Did I really want to leave my family the legacy of having to clear through years of my own rubbish? Didn't they have enough things to do in their own lives? Who's going to clear your clutter if you die or are no longer fit enough to do it? Think about it! If you can't face it yourself, how hard will it be for someone else to do it?

- Will other family members have the time, with their own homes to run, careers to take care of and family to watch over?
- Will distance make it especially challenging for them?
- Will you be expecting them to inherit things that you inherited as well as all of your stuff?
- Will they even realize who features in all the precious photographs or have any idea how much the silver tea-set is worth?

Are you leaving the mess because it's too much work for you to handle on your own? We've just spent weeks clearing things from our home again ready for our move. Will anyone else have time to do this when you're gone? Even simple editing takes time.

If this is your main reason for delaying the job, why not invite family or friends over to help you with specific areas right now? Older children and teens will love the opportunity to help out for cash. They might even take things off your hands. Incidentally, we moved back to the Midlands area using the same removal van we'd used to move to Cornwall. Even though we had the same-sized van, this time it was only three-quarters full. I was very proud indeed!

Passing on inheritance guilt

If you do have important family items you want to pass on to others, perhaps you could consider handing them over now? Your gift might be more welcome if you can share the story behind the items. Do make sure the recipient is interested in the object; your stamp collection might not be of any interest to your skateboarding nephew and your tomboy granddaughter will likely have no interest in your china tea-set! Be prepared for the possibility that your relatives will have no interest in your precious objects at all. In fact, maybe you need to ask the question why are you keeping something just to pass it on? Shouldn't you love and enjoy everything in your home right now? Do you own the item because someone passed it on to you and you keep it out of guilt? Do you want to pass it on to someone else in the future just to "share the burden"?

If you have to pass things on – for example, if you need to move to a smaller house or move in with relatives – try at least to match up items to interests; and now one final word of warning. You might hand the items over with love (and a little background information, preferably written down), but once you have done so the items no longer belong to you. You must part with them along with the words: "Of course, they are yours to do with as you wish, even if the best use for you is to sell them and buy something you like with the money …."

Please do not burden your loved ones with inheritance guilt! After you let things go, it's no longer your business what happens to them! Share them with love – but remember to make them condition-free!

Things that stop you clearing clutter

None of us really need an excuse to avoid doing an unpleasant job, but there are probably strong reasons why you don't want to start. In the end, if you are honest with yourself you'll know these are just more excuses.

- It's overwhelming to try to do it alone
- There is just too much and you don't know where to start
- You can't lift things alone or are not well enough to move things
- Lack of time
- Guilt
- It's someone else's clutter
- You are looking for the perfect new owner for an object
- You have no transport to move it
- It might be valuable
- You're waiting for the ideal place to store it
- It has too many memories attached
- You think you might need it one day
- You think someone else might need it one day
- It has emotional attachments (this is one of the biggest challenges, as we've already seen).

OK, let's look at these issues one at a time.

It's overwhelming to try to do it alone

The simple answer is to ask for help! If you are unwell or unfit, your church, local support groups or even a charity might help you; you might also try roping in younger family members. If you are in good health, please don't wait until you aren't. Remember to pick somebody who is fairly neat and tidy themselves for best results.

There is just too much and you don't know where to start

I know this sounds like it's insurmountable but it's not! I suggest you start with one drawer, one craft collection or a small cupboard (like your bedside cupboard or table). Once you get started it just gets easier; you'll get excited and encouraged by your progress. If you get the urge to start then start. What are you waiting for? Yes, do it now if you feel the urge – put this book down right now! I've been known to bounce out of bed in the middle of the night, run downstairs and put an item out for the charity. This works so well – unless you have to get up early the next day of course. At the very least write down things as you think of them, but doing them right away as the urge takes you is better by one hundred per cent!

You can't lift things alone or are not well enough to move things

As before, the simple answer is to ask for help or task someone else with the job of getting it removed from the property. Many charities would be happy to send someone over to collect your unwanted furniture, and there may be a government-run collection service for large items of rubbish (old freezers, sofas etc.), although there is normally a small charge. Ring to find out.

Lack of time

This is a classic excuse but you made time to buy it/collect it, right? Unravel things at the same speed that you bought them. If you have to, start small. Remove one item every single day. It was how I got started this time round. Use a large plastic box. Our local charity shop donated one to us as people often deliver things in them and they throw them away, apparently. Ours is a horrible pink box that in no way gets confused with the good stuff we are keeping in lovely clear plastic bins.

Place one thing or more in the box every day and then when it's full, take it to the charity shop (or preferably, take it every Monday or Friday or whenever is the best day for you or the charity). Don't leave things hanging around too long or there will be a temptation to retrieve things! (Chinese jug, anyone?)

Guilt

You feel bad because someone gave it to you? You'd be surprised to learn that most people don't even remember what they gave you for your birthday last year, but you should remember that they gave the gift with love and that you are free to do whatever you want with it. Whose knitted tea-cosy is it anyway? I finally started using a body lotion my daughter had bought me for Christmas five months earlier. I really loved it and told her so when I saw her next. She couldn't even remember buying it.

If you don't love it or it's no longer useful to you then pass it on. If by chance the gift-giver happens to ask you about it at some future date, you could:

- Be honest with them about what happened to it
- Say you passed it on as it was now too small, too big or you no longer needed it
- Say it got broken (don't, whatever you do, appear overly upset in case a replacement wings its way over!)
- Say you don't recall what happened to it
- Change the subject!

It's someone else's clutter

I'm afraid this is a common problem but trust me, nagging, moaning and whinging about other people's stuff never works. Nor is it in order to get rid of or sort out someone else's things (even small children's toys) without express permission. Many adults have been left traumatized when Mummy clutter-cleared Mr Rabbit Ears when they were four and he was never seen again! I still get the letters!

OK, so how do we deal with this difficult issue? Surprisingly, people can "catch" the clutter-clearing bug. Once you start clearing your stuff, people around you will begin spontaneously clearing their own things out. Be encouraging! Offer binbags, dustpan and brush, set up the vacuum cleaner on the pipe setting and offer to provide exciting new storage for areas once organized.

You can send organizing video links from internet video channel YouTube to teenagers to encourage them more, and toddlers get quite excited about giving items to the fairies or to children who don't have any toys (a sob story works well with youngsters). Kids copy what you do, not what you say, so get started on your own stuff and watch the magic happen.

Even room-mates and partners will not be immune from your clutter-clearing angel dust. It seems to filter through the air and land on everyone within floating distance. Be excited about your own sorting and organizing achievements and admire any efforts on their behalf at removing unwanted objects from the house. Always praise what they do and never moan about what they don't do. Classic psychology!

I remember one Christmas my young daughters were overly excited about having their very own string and sticky tape (a fun extra present to encourage craft-making). I imagine the gift of their very own duster and polish might have had surprisingly similar results if only I'd considered it at the time.

You are looking for the perfect new owner for an object

Give yourself a time limit; hanging on to objects if you're not doing anything with them is just clutter-holic behaviour! Leave them out on the side where they'll annoy you. Whatever you do, don't be tempted to put them back in a cupboard or attic. Move items with some speed.

You have no transport to move it

As above, ask someone else to move it, call in a charity or the council to help shift it off your property or hire a skip. Once it's full the skip company will take your rubbish away. Donating things is often the cheapest and easiest way of getting rid of something, especially if the other person takes it away with them rather than you having to take it anywhere.

It might be valuable

... But it probably isn't. Check on the internet – a useful source of how much similar items have sold for. Take it to a specialist supplier and ask for an appraisal, or sell on a website with chatrooms where you can talk to people with similar interests. Know that an item is only worth what someone is prepared to pay for it. You can also photograph items and have them appraised online. Do a search or find a helper to do it for you.

I held on to a lot of objects assuming they might be valuable. My furniture trip to the auctions proved that, in fact, most items were worth very little. If you have time on your hands you can have a go at selling items on the internet. eBay can be useful. I've even sold a lot of stuff on Facebook (to similar-minded friends on my "like" page).

There are giveaway sites like Freecycle in the UK (people come and collect your unwanted items for free) and Gumtree (a similar system but here people buy your unwanted items and collect them from your home). If you have loads of CDs or DVDs try using MusicMagpie. com where they buy them. It's easy to put things up for sale on these sites and you even send the items to the company by freepost; then just wait for the money to hit your bank account. A combination of sales and giveaways works best for most people. Since I began writing this book, numerous new companies have appeared on the internet that will buy your old CDs, DVDs and various other items too.

You're waiting for the ideal place to store it

Is this because you want to keep it? If you don't have room for it now you'll probably never have room for it! Think carefully – is this item really clutter in disguise?

It has too many memories attached

This is a dodgy one. Karen Kingston, the author of *Clear Your Clutter with Feng Shui* (the first book about clutter-clearing that I ever read), suggests taking a photograph of the item and keeping the photograph rather than the item itself. Isn't this a fabulous idea? It's helped me out with many a memory-attached item dilemma.

Can you remove part of the item to act as your reminder rather than keep the entire object?

- The key tassel from a large dresser
- A small piece of fabric from a pile of old dresses that once belonged to a deceased relative; or have a few squares of fabric made into something else (a teddy bear, a cushion?)
- One pair of earrings from a whole jewellery box full of things you'll never wear
- A small screwdriver rather than the entire toolkit; donate the rest to a charity or local school
- A pretty jug from the china tea-set; then give the rest of the set away. Just don't keep the Chinese jug you never even liked, like I did!

You think you might need it one day

Ask yourself, "How long am I going to store it 'just in case?'" A month? Six months? A year? Five years? Ten years? Do yourself a favour – give it away and if you ever need one you can hire one, pick one up on sale or borrow it back from your neighbour (whatever "it" is). Small items of rubbish can be even more of an issue. You hang on to a drawer full of elastic bands, old cardboard boxes or silver foil. This stuff will sit in the drawer for five years unused and then you decide to throw it away and within just a few hours your brain will find a use for it (just to prove you right!). Get rid of it! Your mind is playing tricks on you.

You think someone else might need it one day

No! No! No! ... and I repeat, No! What are you, a warehouse? Offer it to the family right now. If they don't want it there will likely be someone somewhere who would be delighted with your old sofa/TV/blender! Please – move it out of the house as fast as you can. Old, slightly useful stuff you don't want is worse than inherited treasure you don't like, so do your loved ones a favour and lose it right now! Don't do the guilt thing either, i.e. "I held on to this because I was convinced you'd want my old 1960s table in your ultra-modern apartment ..." Arghhh! Stop procrastinating and passing the guilt! OK, I'll admit it, we have one daughter's pushbike in the garage and another's old doll's house in the garden shed (but ... they don't have anywhere to keep these in their small modern homes, you hear me protest. Yes, OK, you're right. They have to go!)

It has emotional attachments (this is one of the biggest challenges, as we've already seen)

Oh, I have really struggled with many items that had emotional attachments. These items seem even weirder when you read someone else's list, so here are some of mine.

- The old green glass bottles I dug up myself ... especially the old-fashioned ones with marbles for stoppers (now gone)
- The stone hot-water bottles ... because Mum used to own some (I got rid of them once and then went out and bought two

more ... they've now finally left the nest)

- The Chinese jug I bought when I was ten (yes, yes – still got it)
- The notes my husband wrote to me when we were dating (still have them all but seriously considering a cull – the notes not him!)
- The giant teapot my mum used to bring out when the family gathered round for Sunday tea (it's now used at the retirement community where Mum lives – the perfect home for it!)
- A little wooden toy chair I bought from a jumble sale as a child ... for my Sindy doll (no idea why I kept it but it's in the toy box for my granddaughter now ... she has no idea what to do with it either)
- An angel brooch and a cat painted on a cereal box, both made by my daughter Georgina (yes, I'm keeping them ... but they are in my LOVE pile!)
- A weird clay thing I kept because it was made by hand (have since dumped it)
- Binders and binders full of Vogue magazines I'd had since I was fourteen years old (thrown in the skip to great cheers!)
- Seven folders full of every article I'd ever written (now given to a good cause!) I have the memories in my head and the originals on my computer.

Who's to say why these items become so "sticky", but they do. Break down your resistance one step at a time. Remove objects from their usual home and stand them in a very obvious place where you will see them several times a day (in the fireplace, at the bottom of the stairs – somewhere that you have to keep tripping over them). Give yourself a week to decide. Once you decide put them right in the car (or get someone else to) and remove them from your property immediately!

READER'S EXPERIENCE

I like to think that I'm a minimalist although my material possessions don't agree with me! I'm still clearing out unwanted DVDs and books and selling them. I am replacing them with things that I need to help me live a healthier lifestyle. My possessions must reflect my current needs. Apart from these "things", I actually own very few items of furniture and there is plenty of room to move about in my living area, just the way I like it. I love having space. As far as being organized goes, I really am organized. I know where every item is in my home.

— *GITA*

Free stuff

Are you addicted to free stuff? I think for me it all began with the free gifts in cereal packets. My younger sisters and I would fight over whose turn it was to get the sticker/plastic man-on-a-parachute/collectors card. I think I was also addicted to the gifts that came in Christmas crackers. Did you ever buy a magazine just for the free gift on the front? I know I did ... damn, I did that today!

As an adult I also took home the little bottles of shampoo and soaps from my hotel room and who doesn't crave the free sachets and sample bottles the beautifully made-up women at the expensive cosmetic counters hand over? There is always that hidden promise that "you too can look like this". OK, we all love free stuff but these objects are only exciting until you get them home, and then they just become "tat", rubbish or clutter. We had a massive basket of free soaps and shampoos set out for guests. Did they ever use them? No! It's just as easy to keep a regular-size spare bottle of shampoo and shower gel in the bathroom ready (or even better, a combined shampoo/shower gel that does both jobs).

I also keep one disposable toothbrush in the cupboard (a guest once asked to borrow mine and luckily I had a spare ... phew!). The trouble was, I was so horrified that I might have to lend someone my own toothbrush that I then went out and bought a pack of ten disposable toothbrushes so that I'd never run out. Yes, the trauma created another clutter addiction! But I digress ...

Give the free stuff away or at least use it:

- Package up a bundle of cosmetic samples into a make-up bag and hand it over as a "stocking filler" Christmas gift for a young teenager

- How about actually trying out the sample moisturizer and foundation (I did this recently and even swapped brands afterwards because they were better than my regular brand!)
- Pour the contents of the sample bottle into your regular-sized shampoo/conditioner/bath oil etc.
- Take the free magazine gift to the charity shop (I'm planning on using the freebie I got today ... give me a break, I'm not perfect!)
- Don't buy Christmas crackers.

Use it or lose it

Do you suffer from siege mentality? Have you lived through a war or natural disaster? Do you worry that you'll never have enough water, tinned goods or fuel? It's understandable if this is your reason. My mother (sorry Mum) always had enough food in her cupboards to feed a hundred people in one go – and enough mugs and cups to give them all a drink at the same time (I'm not kidding). I've never lived through a war so I'm not in a position to say.

The sensible thing is to take into account the conditions in your part of the world, keep a small stock of water or whatever you feel you need and recycle it regularly. Keep it up to date and make sure it's kept up off the floor in a clean, dry place so it won't spoil. If you are guilty of a year's worth of stock of items such as toothpaste, shampoo or other toiletries you've hoarded after they were on a buy-one-get-one free offer, stop the madness right now. Donate them quickly!

When you next open a bottle of cleaning product (for you or the house), write down the date you opened it (use indelible marker on the bottom of the bottle or underside of the tube). I bet that toothpaste lasts you five to six months. So that means you'll only get through a couple a year – true? No one needs spares of these items. Once you're nearly out you can pop over to the local supermarket and pick up another one, yes? You may keep one of each product in stock if you have to, but that's it (see how bossy I am getting here!). Toilet rolls are the exception to the rule.

Remember I told you that because I had to share items with my younger sisters as a girl, when I was an adult I would often buy two or three of everything, just because I could. This just became a habit, but one I've now broken (pretty much!).

Spares gone mad

OK, I'll admit it, it wasn't until I seriously began clearing my house that I had any idea how many stocks of things I'd built up. I found five lighters in my study, another three in the lounge drawer, three in the bedroom, three in the kitchen and others dotted all over the house in random boxes. When we cleaned out the shed we found another lighter out there too. Who needs a shed lighter? I now have a jar full, yet I had no idea that I had so many in the first place! We only use them to light candles, although to be fair, we do light candles in several places around the house: the lounge, the kitchen when we eat our evening meal, the bedroom and the bathroom – perfect for those long soaks in the bath. Now I have one in each location – and of course the spares, but at least I know how many I have and won't need to buy any for a long while!

Now that brings me on to candles – yes, I had candles all over the house too. At first I gathered them up and stocked them in one place but, like scissors, this never works. You need your items to be where you use them, so I now have a mini-system of storage in each room for both – one lighter in each of the above spaces and a small, display bowl of candles in each room that we light them in. Yes, and I have a master stock. This may seem over the top to you but it works for me, and everything is kept clear and tidy and I always have the stocks I need to hand. Find your balance; do you have just enough or too much?

Would a mini-system like this work for you? For example, do you paint your nails in the bathroom and also in the living room when you watch TV? Do you need a pen, address book and notepad by each phone in your home? How can you organize your items so that they are neatly stored? More on this later …

Things you might need to buy

Buying things? Yes, this is a possibility now. Once you get clear of clutter you'll find you get drawn into making sure every area of your home works efficiently. When the rubbish is cleared and items are organized you might notice where you have important things missing. Often an inexpensive purchase can make your life run more smoothly. Now you're organized you'll discover what these things are!

> I recently purchased a pair of hairdressing scissors and a comb. I'd never owned a pair and had always cut my fringe (which is normally maintained expensively at the hair salon) with a pair of nail scissors! The hairdressing scissors cost something like £5 from the supermarket – problem solved. In my previously muddled life I just struggled on and didn't even notice.
>
> Whenever I curled up my hair I would section off the piece I needed and the rest of the hair always got in the way. Once I'd cleared my clutter I went out and purchased a couple of small hairclips to hold back my hair. Cost? £1.50! Sorted!

What items are you missing? Are there very cheap little gadgets that will make your life work better? Make a note of them, but don't buy them until after you have cleared space and then see if you still need them. People are often surprised to discover they already own these magical gadgets and had just mislaid them – perhaps you can repurpose something you're not currently using?

Saving things for best

After two incidents, when years ago we were burgled and I lost a lot of my precious china in an accident, I stopped saving anything for best. Maybe you could consider this too? If you have very little storage space, why are you using supermarket tumblers instead of the crystal ones you currently have boxed in the attic?

Treat yourself as if you were a VIP in your own home, but do it every single day. Use your favourite silver napkin ring every day; light that expensive rose-shaped candle before it melts in the sun and wear the exclusive scent to the office before it goes off! So now when you are sorting things into piles of "keep" or "go", maybe you could keep the inherited china and just use it? Breakages happen but wouldn't Grandma prefer you enjoyed her gift rather than simply stored it?

Likewise, wear that silk dressing gown you were saving and wear that fabulous dress to your local restaurant rather than keeping it for some fantasy occasion – it might go out of fashion in the meantime! When I was a girl my sisters and I were each bought a beautiful dress to wear to a special occasion; I think it was a wedding. I recall asking if I could wear the dress afterwards to play in. Of course I was told no because it was for best. Guess what? I grew out of that dress and never did get to wear it again and I still feel bitter about it now! Don't let this happen to you.

I also carefully saved my wedding dress like so many women do (why on earth I didn't sell it to recoup some money at the time I'll never know). We keep them because our wedding is the day we felt like a princess, but on the other hand it's a little odd, if you think about it, to feel the need to store so many things from one day. I had a copy of the invitation, photographs, the dress, the veil, the flowers (silk), a horseshoe from the cake, one of the cakes (for a while!), one of the balloons, confetti and all the cards. Many years later I carefully unpacked my dress from its box. It had turned yellow, was covered in bugs and had been partly eaten by moths! I kept it ... no I'm kidding; of course I threw it away! I still need to sort out the rest of the wedding stuff (I told you, clutter-clearing is a journey!).

Duplicates

Does your home have lots of duplicates? My home was always so disorganized we often bought duplicates of items we'd lost somewhere in the house. We also inherited duplicates and kept them as spares! This "spares" thing really gives off the wrong energy to the universe; it's like saying you don't trust the universe to provide for you. Take a serious look at duplicates in your own home. They have to be earning their keep. As I mentioned earlier, if you use scissors in the bathroom, the study and the kitchen you'll need to keep a pair in each spot, but you probably don't need two blenders and two exercise bikes.

Conjoined/blended families often struggle with this issue, and it's even harder if you're all moving into the home used by one party. If you are one of the growing modern-family variations (mates who share a flat, new partners who move in together and each bring their children with them and so on), who gets to keep their stuff and who has to give their things away? This is why peace often reigns when both parties move out of their old homes and a new, shared home is created.

Gather all of your "duplicates" and decide on which is the best quality, or let the items be decided on a room-by-room basis: for example, she keeps all her favourite kitchen equipment and he gets the pick of the best garage items from among the duplicates (or the other way round). Sell both sofas and buy a new one!

Tchotchke

According to Wikipedia a tchotchke is a knick-knack, a bauble a trinket or kitsch. They should add a better description – it is stuff or clutter. I had never heard of the word until recently, but once I discovered it, it made me laugh and brought back a few funny memories of my own.

I spend a lot of time with my mum and sisters. We are very close and often go to a local garden centre to wander around and maybe stay for a coffee and a chat. The gift shop has some beautiful things but occasionally I wonder if the regular buyer has gone on holiday and been replaced by someone with no taste!

One of us will spot an item, lift it up for others to admire and say, "I love you so much I'm going to buy you this for your birthday ... isn't it gorgeous?" We'll be holding aloft a brightly painted wooden chicken with fluorescent plastic feet and string decoration and the rest of us will fall about with laughter. This week my sister and I wandered around separately and took photos of particularly funny items; we then emailed them to each other on our phones. We could hear each other giggling over the top of the store displays.

We'd cheerfully reply, "I love it! Thank you ... and I'm going to buy you this to thank you for buying it," and a photograph of some equally hideous multicoloured vase shaped like a dog and decorated with rubber flowers would be emailed over in response. We've had a lot of giggles with this game over the years (sad but oh such fun). Sometimes we'll respond by saying, "May I have two of them?" Or, "I love both colour variations" or whatever. Isn't it funny how we recognize some weird objects as weird, yet end up collecting others?

Once, while we were viewing houses for potential purchase I paid particular attention to other people's objects and collections. One house was owned by a police officer and the landing housed a large collection of quirky police-themed figurines: rabbits and dogs with police uniform, toy police cars and so on. Another home had hundreds of bulldog-themed items; they were on everything including cushions, picture frames and mugs. Yet another had the biggest collection of teapots I had ever seen. I sympathized with the owner when she said that she had started her collection with one or two pretty china pots and then people kept buying her more. Eventually the collection included many cheap and gaudy ones that she didn't even like, but the poor woman had no idea how to stop the madness!

Certainly one person's favourite possessions are another person's tchotchkes. When I got home I noticed a few wayward collections of my own: blue and white pottery, cats, china teacups, ducks (I hadn't even noticed that I owned so many), baskets of flowers (both real baskets and images of them) and angels. Angels were decorating almost everything around my house.

Is it time to cull your collections down to the gems only?

CHAPTER 3

Starter projects

"Fill your home with love not stuff."
ANON

When you're faced with years' worth of belongings, getting start-ed on clearing your home can be more than a little daunting. My advice is to start small. Work on simple projects that will spur you on and get your excitement going. The more you do the more you'll want to do. Tiny projects you can complete during the advert break on television or while you're waiting for dinner to cook can give you the little boost you need. Here are a few ideas for you:

Grab-a-bag

Carry a black bin liner around your home and fill it to the top. Make sure you empty wastepaper baskets from around the house too (you might need two bags! Go for it!).

Charity bag/box search

Carry a plastic storage box around the house and fill it with things to donate to the charity/thrift shop. Look in your wardrobe, your clothes drawers and on your shelves for anything that fundraisers might be able to resell.

Tidy your sock drawer!

First tip everything out onto your bed. Dust, wipe or vacuum out your drawer as appropriate and then lay out the socks in pairs. Any sock that doesn't have a matching one has a deadline; leave it a week or two until your washing basket has been completely emptied. Where do those odd socks disappear to? Usually they are lost in the middle of quilts or pillow cases, misfiled or stuck up the sleeve of your sweater!

Let's be honest, it might be a year before they turn up, so decide if you can be bothered to wait and if not discard the odd socks. Check for holes too. Make sure white socks are actually white and throw away any where the elastic has become too loose. I discarded several pairs of socks that simply slipped down every time I was wearing boots! Replacements were cheap and the annoyance went away immediately. Little details like this really ease your peace of mind don't they?

Organize your CD or DVD storage

This is a great one to do during the television advert break. As before, empty the storage out completely. Clean. Organize into piles. When was the last time you played/listened to your CDs/DVDs? Can you give any away to relatives or charities? If you have a large pile to discard remember that CDs and DVDs can be sold online (see the previous chapter and the back of this book for details); you won't make a fortune but it may free up enough to buy something new (not clutter of course!). CDs can be recorded and kept on your phone or computer (back up to be sure you don't lose anything). Then organize your favourites and put back into your cupboard or rack.

Sewing box

I did this while I was watching TV adverts too; it's such a useful measure of normally wasted time. Have a couple of carrier bags handy (one inside the other) for things you want to throw away. Roll up cottons; chuck dirty threads away; get rid of bent pins (you know you have some); find little boxes to organize things into if possible (old acrylic or plastic boxes are perfect, as are small tins). Sharpen sewing scissors.

After my initial sort-out I had a wonderfully organized container, but one year later I found a smaller jewellery box in a discount store and clutter-cleared again into this. Although it was really small, I turned it into a miniature sewing box. It could hold everything I needed (very little, as it turned out!) and I gave away all the spares.

How many reels of cotton do you really need for repairs? Black and white? A needle-case full of pins and needles; a tape measure, pair of scissors and a tiny selection of black and white shirt buttons? Do you keep too much? I know I did.

Cutlery drawer

Tip everything out onto the worktop. Give away duplicates; throw away corks, elastic bands etc. and put pegs and other random items back where they belong. Wash drawer and replace items.

Handbag

This is another great one to do in front of the TV. I organized my own bag with clear plastic ziplock bags; now everything can be found easily and at a glance. Do regular clearouts of paper and receipts, and keep a check on out-of-date make-up etc. You might also consider investing in a lift-out handbag organizer. You organize your contents into the insert and then easily move the insert from handbag to handbag. Voila! This only works with big bags; if you prefer a smaller bag, you could look for one with built-in compartments.

Imagine a friend's toddler tipped the contents of your bag all over the floor in front of a crowd of people. The mother looks on fondly while you blush with embarrassment and terror. Is your bag ready for an audience? Hold this thought as your guide while you sort and throw.

... and briefcase

I bet your briefcase needs a sort-out too. Look out for old files, old diaries, pens that don't work and scrap paper.

Bookshelf

This might be a starter project or a more time-consuming one, depending on the size of your collection. Let's assume for the purposes of this project that you have a small bookshelf full of books. As before, remove everything from the shelves. Dust or wash down the shelves as appropriate – don't forget to clean the tops. Remove everything that is not a book unless you also use the shelves for display, in which case each shelf needs no more than three or five items (two photo frames and a plant? A group of three pots one side and two figurines the other?).

Look carefully at your books one at a time. Sort into four piles: keep, give away, donate, throw. Items you don't want to keep need moving out of the house immediately, preferably right into your car. Then sort your keeping books into categories and display. There is a longer section on books later on.

Medicine cabinet

Wherever you keep your medicines and no matter now organized you are, I bet this area needs attention too. Empty and clean the cabinet and then check the dates on all the products. Remove old prescription drugs (your local pharmacist will dispose of these safely). I like to keep a smaller box with the basic essentials all together; plasters, antiseptic cream and standard painkillers on each floor of the house. One main location might work better for you. Keep medicines up high and, if possible, locked away.

I can't remind you enough how important it is to remove everything from the space and then sort it back into its location. I promise you'll do a better job this way.

Sponge bag

Clean toothpaste tubes and bottles (wipe around the screw lid and outsides of the bottles) and dry off with a paper towel. Remove old bits of cotton wool and cotton buds, old razors etc. Do you need a new toothbrush or sponge bag? Does your razor blade need changing? Check for duplicates. If you have more than one of the same thing, either pour both lots into the same bottle or store one and finish the existing bottle before starting the next one.

Jewellery box

I actually have a vast collection of costume jewellery and it takes up half of a small room, but it's all organized. I display a lot of my jewellery in a lit-glass cabinet and love the idea of browsing my own "shop" each time I get dressed. Jewellery is part of my "love it" collection.

If you have a lot of items to organize I suggest you place a sheet on top of a bed and tip everything on top. Have a carrier bag handy to throw away broken or tarnished items and a small box in which to put old jewellery you want to donate. For example, a jewellery designer or hobbyist might be grateful for your broken pieces – offer them up on Freecycle.

Alternatively, invest in hobby glue to reattach stones that have fallen out (you'll need a special glue that doesn't cloud the surface of the stones). Earring wires can be replaced, you can purchase new earring backs and fastenings can be picked up at hobby shops. It's always worth fixing broken items but, as before, give yourself a time limit. If this is important to you then you'll get it done, otherwise throw. Place pieces in a clear bag inside your handbag so you have them with you when you next go shopping and can ask for advice at your local hobby shop. A small, personally owned shop might be prepared to fix your broken items for you (for a small fee) while you browse around the shop! Ask – you never know.

If you have family pieces that you no longer wear, now is the time to pass them on to others (ask if they are interested rather than assuming or burdening them with items they don't like – inheritance guilt). Alternatively consider whether a specialist jeweller would be able to turn that unwanted brooch into a fabulous necklace! Consider selling your great-aunt's antique earrings and buying something you might actually wear. You know she'd love you to do this! You'll have the same energy but the piece will be bang up to date.

I have jewellery boxes and jewellery rolls to separate my costume jewellery into colours and types, but I also have a selection of shop fittings for keeping much of my jewellery out on display. My haul includes velvet bangle stands (my bargain bracelet buys look a million dollars all arranged together under the lights); display busts and T-bar hangers. Professional shop-display items vary greatly in price, so shop around on the internet for bargains. You can buy leatherette, velvet, wood, cardboard, glass and acrylic. Little metal stands to hang your stud or dangly earrings on cost from just a couple of pounds. Charity-shop bargains like that old birdcage can surely be adapted for more display, right?

Look also to see if you can repurpose other items around your home for storage or display. Old mug trees are great for hanging bracelets and smaller necklaces. Gather cocktail rings together in an old china teacup or sugar bowl; add hooks to a shelf or mirror. Some shops sell jewelled hooks and hangers in the gift section at Christmas (I have several crystal jewel crown hangers and I adore them).

Place pipe-insulating sponge around an old hairspray can (cover in fabric if you wish) and load it up with your bangles. Hook dangly (especially sparkly) earrings around the edge of a cut-glass vase or champagne glass (try your local charity shop for fantastic inspiration or use those inherited glasses you never drink out of). You'll also find vintage ring trees at charity shops and boot sales – or do what I've done and invest in a whole velvet ring pad!

Incidentally, costume jewellery benefits from regular cleaning. Make sure you have silver and gold cleaner for the good stuff and wash gold and silver-plated items in a handful of washing-up liquid and water (or hand soap). Rub the jewellery in your hands with the liquid soap to loosen the dirt and then rinse and polish on an old towel – leave to dry on paper towels before adding to your display or storage. Clean before tidying away.

Keep silver and gold jewellery in small ziplock bags or tissue-wrap safely in your jewellery box. Chunky beads could be hung on a towel rail or toilet-roll holders attached to the wall! Stack your bangles up on a kitchen-paper stand. I have a fabulous inherited cut-glass ships' decanter. It doesn't have any alcohol inside but it makes a wonderful choker-holder for my fancy diamanté necklaces. Get your thinking cap on and if you need further inspiration do a search online using search-words such as "clutter clearing", "professional organizer", "de-clutter" and "dejunk"!

Cosmetics

Again, I have quite a big collection but it's all sorted. Anything that goes round your eyes needs regular throwing out. Never keep your mascara for longer than three months (or even less if you wear it every day). Make sure your eye pencils are sharpened regularly so you always have a clean, new surface and occasionally reshape the top of your lipstick by dragging it along a clean tissue.

Keep your eyeshadow boxes clean by not using the brush that comes free inside. They are never big enough anyway (except in an emergency) so use full-size brushes and keep them all together in old cut glasses, clear glass tanks or pretty pots. You can fill the pots with beads or glass nuggets to separate the brushes. Regularly wash your cosmetic brushes and reshape them back into a point by hand; let them dry naturally. Make sure you have brush cleaner (a professional product used by make-up artists and available at cosmetic counters everywhere) to keep everything clean and prevent eye infections.

I have separate pots for eye-make-up pencils, eyebrow brushes and lip pencils. A couple of shelves on the wall would be fabulous if you have the room, to keep everything safe and out of harm's way. Sort your products into individual bags or baskets or invest in acrylic storage (pots and dividers created for stationery are perfect) or order acrylic storage online. Again, prices vary but the acrylic clear drawers look amazing with all your lipsticks, shadows and lipgloss colours showing through the sides. You'll want to keep them organized and clutter-free because they'll look so pretty and glamourous.

Clear storage is a brilliant trick for keeping things tidy; when everything is on display you want to work just that little bit harder to keep it in perfect order.

Hair products

If, like most women (and some men), you have a huge selection of styling products you'll know how they seem to spread all over the house. When it's disorganized it's easy to buy duplicates of hairspray and straightening sprays. I'm ashamed to say I discovered in my house four hairdryers (including one travel dryer). I found tall plastic drawers on castors in my local discount store and this has turned out to be perfect for keeping my straighteners and curling tongs, brushes and combs all together. With room on top for carrying a basket it's even easier to keep my products all together and I always know exactly what I have and where it is. Because it's on castors I can wheel it into the bathroom if I need to and it also fits nicely into the bottom of a built-in wardrobe.

If you have less room, consider gathering things together in pretty lined baskets or plastic stacking boxes. I like baskets with handles but the trick is to keep your regular everyday stuff together so you only have to move around one item. Keep your "occasional use" sprays and lotions in a separate box and bring it out as necessary.

You might want to keep your hair accessories here too, or perhaps you'd prefer to store them with your jewellery. You'll know the best method for you.

Nail products

If you're someone who would paint your nails if only you had the time, you'll find that getting organized and sorted is the key here too. Most people have manicure products stored all over the house. You'll likely have a nail file in your bag, a varnish in your kitchen drawer and the varnish remover in the bathroom. A manicure system will ensure that you keep your nails in perfect order. First gather together every nail-related product you can find. Old varnish does dry out, so chuck everything that is past its best as well as the polishes that have gone thick and gloopy. Do you have everything you need? This is one of those areas where you might go and purchase a few bits and bobs. Do you have:

- At the very least, a clear varnish, something bright for parties and something more natural for everyday?
- A base coat and a topcoat?
- Varnish remover? (the little pads you can buy tend to dry out quickly but can be useful for travel)
- Files?
- Orange sticks to push back your cuticles and cotton buds to tidy up mistakes?
- A hand cream?
- A small bottle of nail-varnish remover? (I keep a large bottle in storage and the small bottle where I paint my nails).

A small collection of nail products would be fine in a sponge bag. A bigger collection might work better in a divided box. I keep mine in a lidded basket in my living room. Varnish colours are separated into … you guessed it, clear ziplock bags! I use a small tray and paint my nails while I watch television, but if you prefer to do your nails at your dressing table, the storage has to work for its location. Can you dedicate a section or a drawer and organize items into plastic lidless boxes? "Fashionistas" have their varnish colours lined up on racks and narrow shelves (gorgeous, but be careful that it doesn't become clutter).

Keeping things organized means you'll always have exactly what you need – and not too much. Of course if you don't paint your nails then a nail file in your handbag will be sufficient – but don't start buying so many that you just collect more clutter, now, will you?

Perfumes

Perfumes, because they're often received as gifts, can easily become clutter too. If you don't like the smell then you're not going to wear the perfume. If possible give it away (someone will be delighted with it, for sure!). Scents have a short lifespan and light can degrade the contents of your favourite perfume. Having said that, I love to display perfume and enjoy looking at the bottles as well as using the scent.

Gather your scents together – do the sniff test. Do you like the product? Does the perfume suit you? Has the smell "gone off" or does it still smell good? Do you like the bottle? Keep all scents together in a module where you are most likely to spray them (the bathroom maybe, or the bedroom – wherever you get dressed). You can display three or more prettily together on a silver, gilt or mirrored tray. They look great on acrylic trays too – keep scrupulously clean for the best effect. Throw or give away anything you don't want.

Stationery

Have you noticed that stationery also seems to migrate all over the house? How many times do you go in search of a pen or a pair of scissors? My husband and I work from home and each have our own home office; we each keep our own stationery in our offices. John tends to keep his in a divided section in a drawer and much of mine is in…Yes, clear ziplock bags and boxes! I also have a drawer divider and because I rebel against corporate stationery I own a sparkly stapler and jewelled calculator. My sister bought me a sumptuous gold-scrolled sticky-tape dispenser too!

Why not invest in colours and shapes you love? Take your old set to the charity shop or donate to your child's school. I also own beautiful files – why shouldn't you? If you have to store paperwork it might just as well be in something you really like. Existing card files could be covered in pretty wrapping paper or wallpaper, or simply start buying new ones as and when you have the finances. The trouble is that storage too (when old and scruffy) can become clutter in itself. If you love your storage you're going to use it and if you don't – well, you get the picture. Have the best – remember, keep treating yourself like a VIP (very important person).

Because we use pens to write the shopping list we keep in the kitchen I keep a divided basket here too. It's a stationery basket in natural and black wicker but it stores more than stationery – I use the big compartment to store my table mats as well. The two smaller sections contain small squared paper (the sort of block paper you buy to keep next to the telephone) and a pen basket to keep a pair of scissors (black) and a couple of pens (also black). I figure if you have a choice, why not have things matching or colour-coordinated? It looks so much tidier. Yes, for some reason I really do seem to have scissors everywhere (I may have to look at that!).

Plants

Plants as an organizing project? Yes of course! I have plain black, cream and neutral plant pots depending on the room but they all look great together and I sometimes swap them around. Plant pots are not expensive and you can easily get them to match your décor, so why not? Old-fashioned flowery or heavily patterned pots can easily date your room. They are hidden clutter that we don't easily recognize. Perhaps you could paint your own pots or just replace them a little at a time? (or ask for them as gifts). Hand over old plastic pots or those overly decorated ones to charity. Alternatively, do you have a basket you could display plants in? Maybe an antique pot would do the job and fit your décor better? Look at what you already have and could adapt; an old teapot for example?

One fabulous healthy plant can look so much better than half a dozen stragglers. Remove dead leaves, flower heads and stalks.

Change or top up the soil if necessary and feed/water. If all else fails, throw them away and treat yourself to new ones.

Games

Most people have one or two boxed games around the house; a pack of cards, a set of Scrabble or Monopoly; see if you can dedicate a shelf, basket or box and keep them all together. Store them where you're most likely to actually use them (perhaps next to the dining-room table or under the coffee table in the lounge). Check that all the pieces are present (the manufacturer might be able to help you out with missing pieces). Mend any broken boxes and make sure all the contents are wiped clean with antibacterial spray.

Shoes

My shoe project was fairly small but if you have a large shoe collection this might be more daunting. First gather shoes and boots from their many hiding places (in the car, under the bed, in the understairs cupboard …). Do an immediate sweep. Can any go to the charity shop? Have a plastic box handy to put them in right away. Do you have duplicates – six pairs of plain black heels but only one that you wear; have you a bit of a "thing" for brown ankle boots? (Embarrassed laugh!)

Now for the mend-and-throw section. I decided long ago that it was worth paying out to have a favourite pair of shoes or boots reheeled over and over again. Catch them before they get too worn down and damage the shoe itself. Any shoes that need repair, put them in one pile, then place them in a carrier bag and put them right in the car or hang them up with your coat so they go to the repairers the very next time you go into town.

Invest in a tube of craft glue and keep it with your shoes; then whenever a ribbon or jewel or other decorative piece comes off, you can reattach it immediately.

Don't just put all your shoes in a pile at the bottom of your wardrobe; they need better care and if at all possible they should be lifted off the floor (never store anything on the floor if you can help it. It makes cleaning difficult). Built-in shelves or clear plastic shoe racks can be great, but my favourite is the hanging fabric shoe storage you attach to your clothes rail by Velcro (one sticky item you DO want). They suck up such a lot of shoes and take up so little space. You can easily see everything you have in one go, and organize them easily into heel height, summer and winter shoes, colours and so on.

If you must stack your shoes in a box, take a tip from backstage at the fashion shows: take a photograph of your shoes and stick it on the outside of the box. That way you'll know at a glance which shoes you have; your shoes will get worn and not forgotten about. Before you organize your shoes away don't forget to give them a clean and spray with an antibacterial spray (you can buy products specifically for shoes at the supermarket or in shoe shops).

Shoe-cleaning kit

Shoe polish dries up over time, so keep a regular check on it. A small plastic box is perfect for keeping everything together. You'll need a neutral cleaner and maybe some black and brown if you wear these colours. Shoe brushes, cloths for polishing and some glue (see above!). Remove anything from your box that has nothing to do with shoes!

You could of course store shoe-cleaning products with your regular cleaning products but a little hint; if you keep it with your shoes, you'll actually use it!

Magazine storage

Do you have piles of magazines by your bed, under the coffee table and in your car? Let's get sorted! As before, gather together strays and look carefully at your collection. Torn and scruffy magazines can go right in the recycling; neat magazines can go to the doctor's or dentist's surgery, or donate them to your local hospital's waiting room. Decide on one spot to keep them: magazine rack, shelf under coffee table or perhaps a basket. Decide on a reasonable number to keep and stick to it. Each time you buy a magazine, get rid of an old one!

OK, if you must keep a lot at least keep them organized. I usually hang on to only the glossy magazines because they look nicer stacked up on a shelf; you can also consider a magazine box (you'll find them with the other kinds of files at the stationers) and keep one or two boxes' worth on your bookshelf. One box for sports magazines, one for home décor and another for fashion magazines... you get the idea. But be honest with yourself – if you don't regularly browse through them, let them go.

Sort your fridge

Do this on the day before you do a big shop so that food stocks are low and you can work more quickly. Remove everything and wipe down all surfaces with warm soapy water. Check everything for date and decay before deciding what you're moving back into the fridge.

Can you use plastic tubs, baskets and caddies to sort and organize things like cheese, fruit, meat, salad and leftover foods? Look for storage with breathable holes in the side. Label and date items and use food-safe plastics. If you already use plastic trays, give them all a wash or put them through the dishwasher (pop your foodstuffs back in the fridge while you're washing the trays!).

Take the opportunity to test the fridge temperature according to your manufacturer's instructions. If the temperature of food gets too low, they will begin to freeze (and fresh foods will spoil), and too high means the products are not at a safe enough temperature to stop bacteria from multiplying quickly.

The recommendation is usually to put cooked foods on the shelves above raw foods. Keep raw foods like meat and poultry in the plastic wrappings they were purchased in so that you can keep an eye on the expiry date. Keep your fruit and vegetables in the drawers at the bottom of the fridge. Don't forget to wipe down the outside of the fridge when you're done. Good job!

Working with modules and systems

OK, so I've mentioned this a few times. Let's look at this idea in a little more depth. A module is a way of organizing like and similar items together. We've already discussed several ideas earlier in this chapter and if you have a lot of hobbies it's important that you keep your products together. When items stray from the group they get lost and broken and too much time is lost searching for missing items. Worst of all, we may end up rebuying things we already own. The point is that it doesn't take a lot of effort to get sorted in the first place.

Creating little routines and rituals make life so much easier. Here are a few more ideas for you to try.

★ A basket or small shelf by the front door is the perfect place to store your keys and mobile phone (make sure they are safely away from the letter box – you don't want burglars hooking them out). If you have room you could hang a basket next to where you keep your coats, or perhaps put your basket in the kitchen where you could also plug a phone charger. Get into the habit, as we do, of putting your wallet etc. in the same spot each time and I promise you'll never say "Have you seen my keys/wallet/phone/(fill in the blank)?" ever again.

★ Lacking in kitchen-drawer space? Me too. I stitched a tab-hook onto the corner of every tea-towel so that I could hang them up where I needed them, next to the sink. I found old name tags I'd bought for the kids for school and recycled these. As usual I did this job while watching TV and it actually only took me ten minutes. The towels get placed where they belong and never end up on the floor.

★ Not a module exactly but, while we're in the kitchen, here is another idea. We have a magnet on the fridge to pin down the shopping list. Every time we run out of an item or run low it gets jotted down on the list. Loose sheets of paper floating around the kitchen always get lost but the magnet thing works just fine.

★ We keep a shoe basket in the hallway (one with a lid) and each keep one pair of outdoor shoes in it. It's easy to chuck your shoes in as you walk in the door and much less effort than stacking them neatly in a row by the door (who really does that?). The basket does need oc-casional vacuuming but it's an easy maintenance system.

★ Remote controls in our house also go in a basket (I love baskets, as you can see). You can also buy specialized fabric holders and stacking holders for your coffee table if you have a lot of remotes.

Hobby modules

If you like sketching, consider keeping a couple of drawing books and a pencil case full of perfectly sharpened pencils in a box to match your living room (or wherever you're most likely to sit and sketch).

★ How about a pretty lined basket with your embroidery or knitting next to where you sit? (Look for items with a lid if you have a cat – they'll make a bed anywhere you let them.) Crafts need putting away safely from toddlers too – it's amazing how much damage a two-year-old can do with a crayon!

★ Allocate a shelf or space for workout clothes, weights and your yoga mat.

★ If you make jewellery, paint glass or do scrapbooking you'll need more detailed storage for that, but clean, sort and organize everything first. Throw away where you need to before you invest in expensive storage.

★ Most hobbies have specialist storage that has been created specifically for the job, but have a look around your home to see if you can come up with some creative solutions of your own. Many items these days come in expensive packaging and we dispose of so much cardboard each year. Some of it is crying out to be reused. Cut the bottoms off washing-up-liquid bottles to make pots; cover smaller boxes with fabric or wrapping paper and place into larger lined boxes for gorgeous jewellery and cosmetic organization.

★ Gift sets of cosmetics and bath products often come in fabulous packaging. Can you reuse both boxes and lids inside your drawers or on shelves to organize items? Art equipment like brushes, pencils and felt pens look fabulous gathered together in pretty jugs, old vases and even old china. What about that teapot that's missing a lid? I've even planted up winter pansies in old cups and saucers (this is not a good idea for very old or fragile china). Such fun!

★ Beads, crystals and other small hobby items can be gathered in plastic toolboxes but before you invest, check out the unused plasticware in the kitchen cupboard. Can some of this be repurposed for storage? Those extravagant nut chocolates that come in hard, clear plastic boxes (you know the ones I mean) can be really useful too – not that we need an excuse to eat more chocolate, right? Use them for lipsticks and nail polishes for a glamourous display, or use them to organize your jewellery.

Have fun, be creative and think outside (or inside) the box!

CHAPTER 4

How to clear a room

"Be careless in your dress if you will,
but keep a tidy soul."
— *MARK TWAIN*

We have so far looked at the basic clearing method that can be applied to every area of your home. Now we'll go through each room one at a time with more specialist tips and ideas.

Getting help

I think it can be most useful to work with a friend or partner at first. Even children can cast a critical eye over your stuff and offer valuable advice. Your clutter-clearing assistant can be the one who holds the bag or box open and just sits alongside you asking you to explain why you're keeping things – especially if it looks like rubbish to them! Let them be your cheerleader.

If you have to work alone make sure that you feel well and not tired. Being angry about something can actually work in your favour as long as you use the adrenaline to good effect. If you're feeling inspired then go for it – the best time to start is always NOW, when you're feeling in the mood. I've worked many nights through to the early hours.

Playing fast music or listening along to a favourite radio show can help you to feel as if you're not alone. I cleared my whole living room once while listening to clutter-clearing videos on YouTube – whatever works for you is best!

Incidentally, reading a chapter of this book or reading an article online might also act as inspiration. I love to watch organization and storage tutorials on the internet and that really motivates me. Give it a try.

Emotional support

Try to sort through your most personal items when you can get someone else to help you through it. Your helper doesn't need to be a family member. Maybe this is the one area where you could invest in a professional clutter-clearer to help you?

Be prepared to take regular breaks when going through the possessions of deceased relatives. Take it a bit at a time and sort the project into lots of smaller jobs: photographs, jewellery, collectables and so on. If necessary, work with a counsellor at the same time (see your doctor about this) as it's likely to bring up all sorts of emotional issues. If it keeps you awake at night then you may need some help to deal with and get past it.

Keep – throw – donate

Although I'm pretty good at doing this part myself now it can still be helpful to have an assistant for this too. I find it useful if the other person actually places the items into my designated box for me. I can keep my head down and make decisions quickly while at the same time yelling out, "Throw that old thing; yes I'm going to donate this – I already have three the same" etc. The other person can make reassuring noises and congratulate you every now and again, reminding you why you are doing it in the first place. You'll feel satisfied and have someone to share your good work with.

Have separate boxes or a bag system labelled up ready to go. Some organizers suggest three boxes the same but I prefer different types of organization to avoid costly mistakes. I remember once spending a fortune on a set of luxury underwear. It was sitting by the front door in its original carrier bag and at some point someone placed rubbish on top of the bag. The whole thing got carried out to the dustbin – and it was collection day …

- Donate – anything you're not keeping is best gathered in a storage box you dislike, but any gaudy or ugly container will work (just another psychological trick). It will help to remind you that the object no longer fits into your life.
- Throw – black dustbin bags every time.

- Recycle – gather together in a plastic box (green is good as a reminder) and organize afterwards before immediately taking to the relevant recycling centre (a charity shop, say).
- Keep – a nice basket or favourite box ready to carry treasured items around the house to their proper location.

Cleaning essentials

It goes without saying that having plenty of black binbags ready is very useful. There is nothing worse than feeling inspired and having none of the tools to do the job.

As you empty each area make sure you give it a thorough clean inside, on top and underneath. It might be several years before that heavy dresser is emptied completely again so take advantage of this opportunity and move it away from the wall to vacuum behind before moving it back – or into its new position.

Have the right cleaning products for the job

Cream cleaners are brilliant for removing black scuff marks on walls and the black marks in the bottom of plastic sinks. If you need something lightly abrasive this can be a useful addition to your kit; don't over-scrub though, or it will also lift paint off your walls.

Other things on your list should be: washing-up liquid, bleach (use with care), antibacterial spray, warm soapy water, dusters and polish, washing-up cloths, silver polish, wax furniture cleaner and small brushes (old toothbrushes) to get into those hard-to-reach spaces. You'll also want a dustpan and brush, a mop and bucket, a broom and a vacuum cleaner!

Gather all of your cleaning bits in a basket or a plastic box with a handle – of course even your cleaning products should be stored clutter-free and well organized!

A little more about storage...

Once you've cleaned and organized the next step is to consider storage. This is the fun bit but be careful not to rush out and spend loads of money. It's amazing how many things you already own that can be repurposed and reused for different things. Storage needs to keep items clean, sorted and/or displayed, so consider what each item or collection needs and open your mind up to what might work.

- Jewellery for example could be stored in baskets or china bowls; hung from an old spice rack (wall-mounted with cup hooks added) or stored in an antique set of miniature drawers.
- Games (depending on size) could go into a lidded basket, an antique trunk or be stacked on a shelf.
- Toys could be hung from plant basket hooks, piled into old sanded (and painted?) fruit boxes or grouped into brightly coloured fabric laundry baskets.
- Cosmetics could be organized into cutlery trays, wire bins or gathered into a plastic baby box.
- Sort screws and nails into old glass jars (screw or glue the lids to the underside of a shelf) or craft boxes; and hang tools on pegboards.
- Could you hang accessories (handbags, pretty belts etc.) on coat-rack hooks on your wall or add a row of hooks inside your wardrobe to do the same job?

Other ideas

I found a use for old pieces of china and glass to hold small trinkets and rings and earrings.

My set of antique boxes holds packs of playing cards and small games. Wooden boxes store my collection of aromatherapy oils, perfectly protecting them from the light.

Beautifully decorated magazine boxes also gather my notebooks, diary and address books together, keeping them handy but sorted on my desk.

A pinboard on my wall is the perfect place to gather favourite photos and mementos – it's great to have an ever-changing display and as they are "framed" they always look neat.

I like to pull an angel divination card every morning. I keep them in an open dish on my desk so they are handy but neat.

My music CDs are stored in open baskets; you might prefer a proper rack and you can easily pick them up to match your décor;

but sort before you organize. Those movies you received for Christmas five years ago and didn't like; will you ever watch them? Be honest with yourself.

I use plastic craft boxes to organize the inside of my sewing box.

Storage can be clutter too

Make sure you love and use everything you store and, just as important, make sure you love your storage. If your favourite things are gathered together in a dirty cardboard box or pink-stained-from-the-dishwasher-from-the-bolognaise-sauce plastic tub that you hate, it's time to consider something new.

If your storage is damaged then you could probably throw it out or put it out for recycling. If your hat boxes or paper-covered shoe boxes are getting scruffy you might find a lot of use for that roll of leftover wallpaper and a pot of craft glue. Different types of storage can work well but it's useful to keep to a theme:

- All black and white
- Neons or brights (fabulous but you might easily tire of these)
- Themed storage (maybe decorated by you using similar images: trains, flowers, diamanté and so on)
- All wood
- All baskets
- Glass or Perspex jars of various sizes
- Antique pots, china, teapots or bowls for storing stationery, beads, jewellery and so on; but again stick to a theme (pink roses, blue and white for example)
- All plastic, sticking to one colour, all clear or a variety of colours from the same set.

READER'S EXPERIENCE

I've just sorted through my handbag collection so that I can take some of them to the charity shop. The items I found inside included perfume, mints, business cards, theatre tickets, earrings – and money. It was a little revelation! I am now almost £20 richer!

— *AVA*

I hope this chapter has inspired you. Now let's get started!

CHAPTER 5

Organize your treasures

"I want to lead the Victorian life,
surrounded by exquisite clutter."
— *FREDDIE MERCURY*

Once you've cleared your clutter you should be left with only treasures, but all too often your favourite possessions don't get the love and attention they deserve. Is Grandma's china hidden at the back of the cupboard? Are those awards and trophies sitting in a box in the attic? Perhaps it's time to look again at these objects. Are they really clutter in disguise?

If the answer really and truly is "No, I want to keep them," then you and I know that you really need to get the objects out on display … or even better, as in the case of Grandma's china, use it! My grandmother bought me a set of six china cups and saucers for my twenty-first birthday. Now I'm fifty but those cups and saucers have been used almost daily. Sure, I lost two cups at some point but it doesn't really matter. Those objects were given for me to love and enjoy them and I've had nearly thirty years' worth of enjoyment out of them. Of course I could have kept them safe in bubble-wrap at the back of the cupboard but what would be the point of that?

Look at it today, make your mind up today! Sometimes your clutter is just a decision you've been putting off, so decide.

If you have precious items that you want to use but are worried about them being lost or destroyed, consider the following:

- Take a really great photograph of the object. If you lose the object you'll have the photograph for ever.
- Make sure items are properly insured.

- Display them somewhere safe (in a lit cabinet? In a jewellery box?).
- Be sensible about their use – don't give your best cut glasses to the children (although I used to and my children never broke any).
- Don't put your favourite items in the dishwasher or the washing machine (wash by hand). I'll admit I stick most things in the dishwasher but that's just me! However, once you have decided which precious items to keep, clean them carefully and look after them.
- Make sure your antique jewellery has a safety chain fitted (a good jeweller will do this for you). Don't wear that precious necklace until you get the clasp fixed (be sensible about it).

Then, once you've taken precautions, use and enjoy the items that you love. Granddad would have wanted you to have worn his gold pocket watch occasionally or at least to have it placed in a beautiful display box where you can enjoy it every day.

The China Cabinet

When I was a little girl I used to visit my father's aunts with my parents and sisters. Us girls were fascinated with the "front room", a room that was never used but which just always held a collection of the most precious items the family owned. I always wondered why the room was not used even when we, the family, would visit! Most of all I was intrigued by the "china cabinets"; always a glass-fronted cupboard with shelves full of "special items". To be honest, the objects were not really that special (in my eyes) but I guess if you have lived through a war then everything is precious!

I inherited some of these objects: a favourite set of three Chinese blue- and gold-edged cups and saucers, three plates and one dinner plate (the set was split among several relatives). I do love these and they made it through my own cull. I've had the plates out on display for many years too but the secret is to actually use them occasionally! Other items included holiday mementos – the very worst of "Welcome to … [insert holiday destination here]" tat! No thank you! Even chipped china (and pottery) ornaments were included in this most precious of cabinets; theirs not mine, I mean. I always throw something away once it is chipped or cracked (check the value first as some antique pieces are still worth some money if you want to sell them).

Rather than discourage me, as an adult during the height of my clutter addiction I filled not one but two cabinets full of items of my own. The china and crystal glasses were mainly for display; I didn't want to use anything in case it got broken. Big mistake! I had so much stuff piled upon the shelves that one day, while sitting watching television, I heard an almighty crash. The top shelf had smashed down onto the shelf below and this in turn had brought down the middle shelf. Worst of all, I knew that opening the glass-fronted doors would only break more things!

I was devastated by the loss and you'd think that would have been the end of the matter but it wasn't. Several months later I heard another crash. This time it was the shelves on my corner unit. The same thing had happened again and more items were broken beyond repair! Lessons learned here?

- Too many items … can be too much!
- Use display shelves for a small selection of items, not everything you own.
- Don't over-stack shelves of any sort.
- Make sure shelves are secure – they can even be a hazard if you are not careful.
- Items can get broken even when you're not using them, so use and enjoy!

Years ago one of my sisters had a row of pine shelves at picture-rail height around the top of her living-room walls. The shelves had been badly hung and one day one of them came tumbling down. It was above the sofa and contained lots of heavy items including several old-fashioned stone hot-water bottles and old-fashioned green glass bottles. Luckily no one was sitting underneath at the time (it happened during the night) – honestly, someone could have died. I cannot repeat enough, do not overfill shelves for display!

If you have a lot of items that you want to display, consider keeping a couple of boxes in a garage or attic (yes, yes I know I told you earlier not to do this!). You don't have to have everything you own lining your walls at one time and it's OK to have a small selection of things to display if you rearrange regularly. (Note I did say a small selection.) Swap your displays around from time to time. Of course if the "spares" never get brought back into the house you have to reconsider whether or not they are precious! Keep reminding yourself of the "rules".

READER'S EXPERIENCE

I am currently in the process of packing boxes because we move in three weeks' time and I have taken this opportunity to have a really good sort-out; it feels very cleansing. A lot of "stuff" has gone to family and friends as well as to the charity shop. We're only taking what we need to our new home; there is no room for clutter any more in our lives.

— *CATHY*

Photographs

I have found my photographs to be one of the hardest things to organize. I've done it several times over the years. At one point I had piles of albums and several boxes of photographs. When we did our last move I took out every single photo from the boxes and albums (yes, I stripped out the already organized albums) and laid them on the floor (a bit at a time). Even the "sorted" things still need editing from time to time.

Here are some great ways to sort your photographs:

★ Get rid of photographs of people you don't like. I had pictures of an old family friend. She used to make me feel bad about myself and I had already dropped her from my life many years ago, yet I was amazed at how many photographs of her I still had in my albums. I removed the photographs and shredded them one at a time. It was extremely cleansing – and healing!

★ Immediately throw away torn photographs, those with scratches, duplicates and photos where someone's thumb or hair sneaked into the photo.

★ Gather photographs of each person together (not your immediate family but friends and more distant relatives). You'll likely find that the people you don't like so much have a smaller pile of pictures! Can you choose your favourite photograph of each person and keep only that? Do you honestly need more than one photo of each person?

★ I had a massive collection of photographs of my nieces and nephews (whom I love dearly, I might add). I kept several photos of each of them but made a rule that I would sort and keep them by year/age so that I had maybe a couple of each of them as babies, a couple each of them as toddlers and so on rather than the pile of fifty I started with. This forces you to keep only your favourites. Be discerning.

★ Do you have photographs of scenery? If you don't recognize the view in the picture, the photo has to go! If it doesn't bring back any memory there's no point keeping it. If you have ten photos of the view – well, you get the idea.

★ Old pictures of people you used to work with? They could probably be thrown away too, unless they are still dearly cherished friends of course.

★ What about photographs of yourself you don't even like? Who the heck needs to keep those?

★ If a picture makes you feel sad, get rid of it (but keep the good memories in your mind).

★ At first I scanned a lot of photographs. Back them up regularly on your computer if you're going to rely on this method alone.

★ Be honest: if there was a fire and you lost all of your images, are there friends and family that could replace enough of them so that you felt you had a "good enough" collection?

★ Play games with yourself like, "keep the best 100 photographs". Put them into one album.

★ If you have lots of photographs of a particular person and feel bad about throwing them out, give them away! I laid out a series of envelopes on the floor with different people's names on and sorted my photos into the envelopes by name. They were delighted to receive photographs of themselves that they had never seen. Don't forget: tell people you don't want any of the photographs back. If they don't want them then they are welcome to give them away too, or throw them as appropriate! Funnily enough, some people didn't want to keep the images of themselves that I gave back – even they didn't like them!

★ Don't keep photographs just in case someone else might like them one day. Your own children won't thank you for a massive pile of photographs of people they don't know. One small album each of photos of themselves and family members is probably more than enough.

★ Make sure every single photograph that you keep is labelled, not just with the name of the person but when the photograph was taken and why. If they are relatives don't just write "Aunty Sue", make a note of whose aunty she is and on which side of the family. Every image must have the name of the person, when and where it was taken and the date or the age of the people in the photograph. Add a sticker to the back with the information typed up if you use a computer; you'll find it easier. Over the top? Not if you are leaving the images for future generations!

★ …Which brings me nicely to my next point. We have piles of ancient photographs of my husband's family and we have no idea who they are! It's such a shame. If there is no one left to identify them – let them go! (Unless you are crafty and could reuse glamourous black-and-white images in some way; decoupage a tabletop and place glass on top? Create a family montage photograph by gluing all the images together under one frame?) Or not – don't go looking for reasons to keep them; and certainly don't let me persuade you.

★ If you want photographs to make a family tree, maybe now is the time to sit down with one of the online registries and add images, dates and information about your ancestors. Give yourself a deadline (say six months) to get this done. It may be welcomed by future generations. If you're not going to find the time to do this, maybe there is another family member who would be interested in carrying out this task?

★ Children are brilliant at sorting out photographs – ask for their help! Maybe even pay them, especially at the end when you're ready for images to go into albums. Teenagers might happily be bribed into scanning your favourite images.

★ I did a lot of my photograph-sorting while I was watching television (surprise, surprise) – it seemed less of a chore some-how. All the photographs were in large (very large!) plastic boxes and each night I tackled a couple of hundred.

★ Photograph-sorting can be exhausting. Working your way through your life brings up all sorts of emotions. Try to have regular breaks and don't do too much at once. A glass of wine might help.

★ Have an initial sort-through of images and put them away. Set a diary date to come back and go through them again. I promise there will be photographs that you thought you wanted to keep that you are now ready to let go.

★ Organize your images by date (roughly) or activities and remember, only keep the best ones.

What to do with the photographs you are keeping

★ Make yourself a top 50 album. Everyone has images that they feel really tell the story of their life. I have some beautiful ones of my daughters (although I am a grandmother too now). Amongst my favourites are my girls standing in a sunflower field, the girls holding hands on the front lawn at my mother's house wearing summer dresses and straw hats .... When I examined the photographs and was really honest with myself, there were really only about fifty that I wanted to go into that "really special" album. Imagine you were told that you had to move to a new home and you could only take strictly fifty photographs with you. Which ones would you take? Would thinking like this help you to sort more seriously?

★ Add your favourites to your mobile phone's photo album so you can enjoy them right now! Make a mini-album to carry with you or use credit-card size self-sealing plastic sleeves to add a couple of pictures back to back to carry in your purse or wallet. I sized a couple of pictures (one of my parents and another of myself with my sisters), laminated the two photos together and then gave them to my sisters as Christmas presents. They were a big hit.

★ Can you turn your favourite current image into a drink coaster, magnet or key-ring? Ask at your local photographers to see what products they currently produce. Do be careful that you're not just bringing in more clutter of course!

★ Consider a plug-in photo frame where you add your images electronically; you can add as many pictures as you like and they run as a slide show.

★ I have a small selection of photograph frames and every time I had a new photograph of someone I wanted to display I simply went out and bought a new frame. The collection just grew and grew – voilá ... clutter! Now the frames hold pictures of certain people (or a family group) and each time I get a new, more up-to-date image, I just swap the images in the frame. Simple really (so why didn't I always do this?).

★ Consider buying a new set of albums (or just one gorgeous album). Make it something that you are happy to keep around in a place where you will look at it often. Scan any other photographs you want to keep and then give the originals away.

These days with digital photography, people only print their very favourite photographs. That makes a lot of sense, but don't let your digital collection become clutter too. Make regular clearouts to keep on top of it all. When you're out and about, ask yourself, "Am I so busy taking photographs I've stopped enjoying the activity?" *Be* in the moment; don't just wait to enjoy the event afterwards with your snaps.

Books

OK, I know we've already discussed books but this section is for the serious collector! Over the years I've owned thousands of books. Maybe it's because I am an author that I'm so interested? Years ago I worked as a temp in a library at the technical centre of a large brewery in Burton-on-Trent. Even though I wasn't especially interested in beer as a subject, I still loved looking after the books. It was one of my favourite jobs ever.

Treasured books, your favourites and those that were given as presents, seem to glow when you look at them. It doesn't matter if they are old or new. Old books, on the other hand, that you've never read (and probably never will), have a different energy about them

– they feel stagnant and dead. The joy of clutter-clearing your bookshelf is that once you've finished, the whole shelf of special books you keep will have that magical glow about it.

You'll need to keep your collection under control. Make yourself some rules; for example, every book you keep has to fit onto the bookshelf you already have. Or maybe you decide that each time a new book comes into the house, an old book has to leave. If you seriously can't get rid of any more books, at least make sure they all have a home. Books on floors, staircases and cupboard tops make for a dusty and dangerous hazard.

Here are a few ideas for sorting your books:

★ Go around the house and gather up every book you find. You know the routine now. If you are a book fan you'll likely have them hidden everywhere. Mine were piled in the bedside cabinet, on the bedside cabinet, under the bed, in windowsills, piled on side tables, stacked on my sideboard and in several cabinets and bookcases.

★ Place them on the floor in a different room (not the room where you have your bookshelves). Have some large plastic boxes handy – these are for books to give away (you might want to throw the odd damaged book but in most cases the books can be given to a good home). Work alongside someone else if you can. It helps to have someone else to pass things to. If you're alone, play some fast music so you keep up a good pace. *First go through the books one at a time. Make a decision immediately – initially put them in "keep" and "throw" piles.*

★ Then start to sort your books into piles of similar subjects. My categories were things like self-help books, angel and afterlife books (research for other books I have written), and craft books, novels etc. You'll have your own collections.

★ I decided not to keep any paperback novels once I'd read them. How about you?

★ Next I looked over my book piles more critically. How many books do I need on each subject anyway? Even my reference books were given a cull. Do you actually research using your reference books or do you, like many people nowadays, really prefer to find the information on the internet? Think about it!

★ If there are books you haven't ever read, get rid of them.

★ If there are books you haven't read but you really want to read them, transfer them to a different pile – they can have their own shelf and if you still haven't read them within a certain number of weeks or months consider taking them on holiday to read. Still not read them? You know what to do!

★ One rule I learned: just because someone else gave you the book and personally signed it (even if it was the author), there is no rule that says you have to keep it once you are finished with it. Whose house is it anyway?

★ Now for the final check. Pick each book up again one at a time (yes this is time-consuming if you are a book hoarder!). Look at it carefully. Does the book glow with anticipation or excitement? Does owning it make you feel great? OK, then it's a "keeper". If not then place it in your get-rid-of box.

★ If you can't decide on any book then it's really not a keeper is it? Tell yourself, if you really want to read the book again you could always borrow it from the library, or if the worst comes to the worst you could buy it again. In all the years I have done this, only twice have I rebought a book I gave away.

New homes for old books

Don't automatically throw your books. I like to avoid adding to land-fill whenever possible and books nearly always deserve a good home elsewhere. Here are just a few ideas.

★ Charity shops love your old books. Or consider donating to the next school jumble sale.

★ Old books might have value. Take them to a second-hand bookstore to sell (but don't use this as an excuse to hang on to them "until you have a chance to take them". Remember the rule: give yourself a time limit to do this and if you don't, take them to the charity shop.

★ Sometimes libraries will be interested in taking new, hardback books in excellent condition. Check with your local library.

★ If you have the time and energy, try selling books on the internet. If you don't have the time, pass the whole pile over to a teenager and get them to sell them for you, promising them half the proceeds. You'll need to consider postage costs and padded bags for sending things out (it's a time-consuming job).

★ You can sell books at car boot sales too but don't expect more than 10p–50p even for books in the very best condition. String together sets of books for more money or place them in a box with a poster saying "Five books for £1" or similar amount. We also had success with stringing together piles of similar glossy magazines (homestyle and fashion magazines). Tie on a label with one price for a set.

★ I had a massive collection of alien and UFO books (I know, it was a phase I was going through). I had success selling large sets of similar books to other collectors on eBay; you'll probably get more money selling things one at a time, but to be honest I couldn't be bothered; it can take a long time!

★ If you have specialist books for a particular hobby, try selling to like-minded friends on the internet in chatrooms and similar sites. I sold loads of my old spiritual books to Facebook friends and we all benefited. I was delighted to pass items on to people who would treasure them and they had the benefit of getting books kept in excellent condition at well below usual cost. Everyone wins.

★ If you have carrier bags full of old novels, check to see if your local retirement home would be interested in taking them off your hands.

★ If you have finished with the very latest releases, a second-hand bookshop (especially one in or close to tourist destinations) will probably buy the books off you for a reasonable fee or give you a certain point-value so you can take some books away in exchange for the ones you donate.

★ Do you have a neighbour or friend who is unwell or bed-bound? A pile of romantic fiction might make her day or month, while she is recovering.

★ Doctor's surgeries, dentists, hospital waiting rooms etc. would love your old magazines (if they are in good condition), and they might take children's books too.

★ Place a free ad or postcard in your local corner shop offering your books for collection on a first-come-first-get basis. List a few of the general categories. Let someone come and collect them, saving you petrol too.

★ Ask friends if they have need of new-condition books as prizes for charity raffles.

★ Give away hobby books to a local club and children's books to a local playgroup or school.

Books you're keeping

★ Make your own rules of course, but I decided to only keep one book by my bed (I cleared my drawer to keep it in, so it's actually hidden away), then I have one spare book in the cupboard below. The rest of my books are on bookcases (I have three but two of them contain books I am using for research for work). See how I made an excuse there? The hoarder is always on a journey!

★ Don't overcrowd your bookcase. Stack some sideways on and others piled up for interest. Add a plant or two and a photograph frame or similar to make the shelves look more interesting.

★ Remove scruffy slip covers.

★ Keep organized and store books of similar subjects together.

★ Use bookends; useful for dividing your book collection into smaller sections.

★ If you have a lot of books consider creating purpose-made bookshelves over doors, in alcoves and under the stairs. Bookshelves are narrow and don't take up a lot of room if you make them to fit available space, rather than buy purpose-built free-standing shelves that might not fit.

E-Readers (for electronic books)

I have been buying most of my new research books as electronic books or "ebooks" as they are usually known (I have a Kindle reader). I wasn't sure about using this new technology at first but now I love it. It's so much easier to read books in bed on a reader! When I'm clearing my bedroom or putting on my make-up I use the "voice" facility so that my books are read to me directly from the machine – you soon get used to the robotic-style voice (check when you buy ebooks to see if they're voice-enabled). It's great for when I am exercising too. I hate to work out but it's made a lot easier if I can listen to my books at the same time. It does use up the battery more quickly, but it's easy enough to recharge when it runs down.

E-readers are a massive space-saving tip. Even if you read only on holiday it is much easier in terms of space to take your ebook reader, cover and charger than it does to pile six new novels into your case. You can download new titles instantly, even while your plane is sitting on the tarmac, and you can house thousands of books on one tiny piece of equipment. My reader is lighter than most paperbacks and about the same size. Don't get me wrong, I love my paper books but I got used to the e-reader really quickly – it's a great alternative. If you're a book-oholic too, why not give it a go?

As I don't store and keep my novels after I have read them, this is the perfect way of storing my holiday reading. If you don't want to store and keep books, it could work very well for you too. It means you don't need to sort and get rid of books once you've read them; and best of all, you never feel the need to stock up on several books in advance "just in case" you ever get the time to read them, because you can download books one at a time as and when you need them. As an added bonus, ebooks are often cheaper to buy (although in the UK, unlike printed books, ebooks do have VAT, sales tax, added on).

Collections

Now let's move on. How do you manage your collections? I suggest you discourage well-meaning friends from adding to your collections. You know how it is – you start with two or three antique china teacups or items in a particular colour or pattern that you rather like and before you know it, someone thinks you collect any sort of teacup and suddenly you're getting cheap pottery – gaudy cups in every colour imaginable. Don't keep items out of guilt! When people admire your treasures make it clear that you don't like other people buying things for you; I'm sure you can find a way of being polite!

Sometimes collections can get out of hand. I remember one of my sisters started off with a couple of frogs and eventually they started to take over the house. They were on everything: tiles, plant pots, cushions.... Sometimes you can even stop collecting an item but others continue to buy things for you years after you've discontinued liking them! Take my advice: to be on the safe side, don't collect anything at all!

Muted and harmonising colours are less messy. Plain can be neater than patterned, but don't let that stop you displaying items that give you pleasure. When I am working on a book I need lots of stimulating objects around me. I remember one summer when I was researching a book about fairies; I replaced the net curtain at the window in front of my desk with a green and purple "magical"-looking sheer panel. I filled my windowsill with crystals, shells and natural objects as well as several fairy figurines that sat on plant pots! Once the book was finished I removed the whole lot; I needed this particular inspiration for only as long as I was writing my book. Do you need inspiration to work with the current phase of your life? Let your object move to a new home when you've moved on.

Do you have inspirational items around your home that you still keep, even though the ideas they gave you are long since incorporated into your life? Do you have objects that were relevant for the person you used to be or hobbies that are no longer of interest to you? Perhaps these can go now?

Arrangements

I always fancied one of those tables with the clear glass top and the space below for displaying treasures; a boxed frame on legs. You find them at old manor houses owned by the National Trust. Of course there are modern-day equivalents; wall-mounted shadow boxes and bargain glass display units with lighting above. These can be really useful.

Interior designers will often display items in matching pairs; it signals togetherness. One candlestick on each side of the mantelpiece or two ducks on the window ledge reminds us of a happy life pairing, two people in love. Larger items are better displayed alone. One fabulous vase on a corner shelf can have way more impact than twenty trinkets jumbled up together. If you have a larger collection to display, and they're all different sizes then odd numbers can work better. Florists work in threes, fives or sevens; it simply looks better.

If your collection contains lots of tiny items they might look better under glass. Make sure they're well lit. If you truly love something then look after it. Do you have time to keep your possessions washed or dusted? If not, think again as to whether they really deserve a space in your home.

★ Organize your displays using similar colours or themes.

★ Allocate a space for your collection and stick to it. Don't let your stuff take over so much space that you begin buying more and more storage to keep it in – or, in my case, building an extension to the house!

★ Pictures often look better when hung over the top of a piece of furniture; it seems to anchor them better. This works with mirrors too; over a mantelpiece or side table, for example. Don't hang too many together or you'll not appreciate any of them.

★ Can you edit your collection? Is it time to get rid of your less valuable pieces or the cheaper items in your collection that you bought when your interest was at its peak? It's easy to get carried away when you're in collection mode and buy anything and everything that is related to your subject. Trust me, I know! If I was in a painting phase, for example, then I needed every bit of "kit" available to go with my collection. When I took an interest in cocktail rings I was buying every ring in sight – especially when they were in the sale.

★ By all means enjoy your collections when they are current and your interest is high, but when you're ready to move on to a new hobby or collection make sure your old hobby is ready to move on too.

Unwanted gifts

Once you start to work your way through your clutter you'll want the neat areas to stay neat. Holiday and celebration gifts can be a challenge. You stop buying things yourself but like the teacup and frog collections we discussed above, other kind-hearted people keep buying you things that you don't want. One tip is to take a photograph of yourself wearing or holding the gift and send it on to the person concerned. You might also (if you really have to) make a note of using the item or wearing the object when they come to visit – once only. Then let the item go to someone who would love it.

More storage and organizing ideas

If space is at a premium, you have to be extra clever with your storage solutions.

★ How about creating a window-seat with a lift-up lid or sliding doors? Use it to store pre-organized items in clear plastic boxes so you can find things easily. This type of storage is useful for sleeping bags (sealed in zip-up clear bags) and things like cushions for your outdoor furniture. Be careful not to use it as a hidey-hole to throw things into when visitors call unexpectedly.

★ Consider a coffee table with drawers or space for baskets (yes, my beloved baskets!) for your living room. Bedside cabinets with drawers or a cupboard space are more useful as a lamp table than a plain side table with no storage. We've recently purchased a new coffee table and specifically looked for one with a shelf underneath to store magazines neatly.

★ If you have space next to your fridge or freezer, this is ideal to build in wine racks or to hang hooks to keep your brooms, ironing board or fold-up clothes airer.

★ Add a row of hooks inside built-in cupboards for outdoor coats, jewellery, aprons and things like tea-towels.

★ Items displayed on the wall are always less messy than things stacked on the floor. Can you add a wall-mounted cupboard or attach a free-standing bookshelf to the top of a cupboard to create a type of dresser? Paint both halves to match.

★ If you're short of wardrobe space, check out manufacturers of built-in wardrobes to see if their interior fixings for storage of shoes and so on can be worked into your existing wardrobes. Shop around for the best prices or, even better, wait for the sales before making expensive purchases.

★ Look out for fabric storage to maximize your internal wardrobe space, including those hanging shoe racks we talked about earlier. It saved me so much space when I added one of these to my own wardrobe. It had the added bonus that I began wearing shoes that were previously hidden in a jumble at the bottom of my wardrobe – and as they were stacked in pairs, I never lost another shoe. Bliss!

★ Many stores sell coat-hangers that will double, treble or more the amount of clothes you can hang in each space. These specially designed hangers have hanging space for several items of clothes at once, with the hangers stacked up one over the other.

★ If you must store things under your bed, consider lidded plastic boxes with rollers. This is the ideal solution for storing spare bedding, towels and out-of-season clothes. Label the boxes on all sides.

★ If you have deep, dark understair cupboards, add a light to the inside so that future clutter has nowhere to hide. Bring in a professional electrician to install it for you or look out for a battery-operated light. Use it to store your vacuum cleaner, but make it a rule that everything else has to go into clear plastic boxes with rollers so you can easily see what's stored inside – and, more to the point, easily bring it out to use it.

★ Add baskets to the wall inside your hall closet; one each for gloves, scarves and outdoor hats. Perhaps this is a good place to keep suntan lotion and sunglasses too?

★ Can you attach speakers, radios and televisions to the wall on hinged brackets? Again, this frees up valuable surface space. See if this is practical in your home and again, for safety's sake, ensure they are fitted by a professional.

★ If you get a choice (and we did), look for a home with wide windowsills. It's amazing how you suddenly have more storage space! A vase and a plant don't overclutter a sill but they make clutter-free space on your bookshelf.

★ We have an old metal pan rack in our utility room. We stopped using it for pans a long time ago but it fits nicely into the gap between the washing machine and the freezer and stores the boxes of cat food and cat bowls. Can you repurpose a pan rack this way? Or maybe you have an old spice rack that would be perfect to display smaller collections of nail varnishes or jewellery? What items do you already have that can be reused elsewhere? Keep checking and save money.

★ Companies sell all sorts of clever items for organizing your kitchen cupboards. Look out for racks and metal shelves that you can use to stack jars more effectively, or use a stepped organizer for tins. It doesn't take much effort to display similar tins together on a shelf, and this is more useful when taking stock of your supplies. Years ago I was a trainer for a large supermarket. In shops they always teach the staff to face the labels to the front and I've done this ever since in my own cupboards.

★ A rotating circular shelf, sometimes called a lazy Susan, is the perfect thing for a corner cupboard or higher shelf. You can easily rotate an item to the front of the shelf to save lifting everything out to find the thing you're looking for.

★ If you're buying a new footstool or ottoman, look for one with storage underneath. It might be the perfect place to keep your knitting, newspapers or the remote control.

★ I keep a small laundry basket (with a lid) in my little sitting room to keep my granddaughter's toys in (she has more toys in the understairs cupboard in clear plastic storage bins). Baskets always look nice for storage in a living area (I hate plastic storage on show but it is fabulous in cupboards). It also keeps the toys under control and is easy to clean up after use. You can always rotate the toys, as I do. Not all the toys need to be out in one go.

★ In our current home we fitted in most of the furniture well but we did end up with a chest of drawers with no home. Luckily it was waxed pine and matched my living-room furniture, so we decided to move it there. I added a lamp on top, a plant and some photo frames and it now looks quite at home. It is a great place to store tablecloths and spare candles but I'll be honest, it also has some empty drawers! I'm thinking it might be a great new home for craft supplies as the drawers are deep and spacious. [Note – since starting to write this book I've decided the chest of drawers was clutter too and so I sold it!]

★ CD and DVD collections can easily get out of hand. We buy our movies thinking that we'll watch them again but the truth is we probably only watch twenty per cent of them more than once. Sell the part of your collection that you no longer need and consider subscribing to a movie channel of some sort. It will probably save you a whole stack of money too.

★ Consider backing up your music on your computer and selling on the originals.

★ If you don't have a lot of room for that home office, consider creating something built in. If your desk or computer table pulls out from the cupboard and you can close the door on everything at the end of the day, you'll be able to double up the use of your existing rooms. My mother had a fabulous computer cupboard that matched her bedroom furniture but after use closed neatly away. How can you adapt your current home office or make one? Or simply create your office along a wall and put sliding wardrobe doors in front.

★ If your storage doesn't match, consider making a new cover or spray-painting so that everything blends in together. It looks neater.

★ Can you make use of professional (hotel/shop) storage to organize the things in your home? If you make hot drinks in your bedroom, or your bedroom doubles as a bedsit, how about a little tea storage tray or rack to keep your drinks on?

★ Would a café or hotel-reception-style magazine wall rack work in your home for your magazines and newspapers? Or maybe a small basket or box with your most used bathroom items would work for you in your bathroom in the same way they lay these out in hotel bathrooms. How about gathering items in an old champagne bucket?

★ Is it worth investing in a bathroom sink with a built-in cupboard beneath, or perhaps you could get a carpenter to make one to fit your existing sink? I love to see clear bathroom surfaces – who needs to display the bleach and underarm deodorant? They certainly don't add anything to the décor, do they?

★ Wall baskets can be really useful for bathroom products, or put up a shelf and line up tall tubs to keep your deodorants, spare soaps, toothbrushes and so on hidden away. There is nothing worse than sprays and lotions piled around the sink or cluttered in the windowsill.

★ Look out for free storage like plastic ice-cream containers after use. Label up and use to keep your craft items in.

★ If drawer and cupboard spaces are at a premium, have a look around your home to see what you can reuse to get organized. If, like me, you had piles of old candle jars (which you had washed, hoping you'd reuse them for something), then put a few inside a drawer to organize drawing pins, paper clips and elastic bands. They are perfect for cotton buds and hair clips too.

★ Cardboard display "outers", the decorative packaging often used for perfume gifts at Christmas, are usually too pretty to throw away; but if you're not careful they can easily become clutter too. However, if you lay the open boxes inside a drawer they are perfect for organizing the contents. Big boxes can be used to store spare make-up (label the outside clearly).

★ Stationers sell metal or plastic label holders that you can stick to the outside of a box and slide in a card that you've pre-labelled. Alternatively, add a parcel label (punch a hole in the side and tie the label on with string), for a beautifully rustic look. This works well on jars too. Check out stationers for self-laminating business-card holders for another way of creating pretty labels. Place a strip of pretty paper at the back and glue a smaller label to the front (so you have a decorated border all round), then seal the whole thing inside the plastic and stick to the box.

★ Add spare shower hooks or metal S-shaped hooks to a wardrobe rail and use to hang your handbags inside.

★ A dish-drying rack might be just the thing you've been looking for to organize your children's colouring equipment. Add colouring books, crossword puzzles, dot-to-dot books etc. in the plate compartments and keep pencils, crayons and felt pens in the plastic knife and fork pots.

★ Clear acrylic toothbrush pots are a great way to sort kids' crayons and pencils into different types or colours, or use bright mugs, the sort you often get free with Easter eggs. Keep them tidy by adding them to a high-sided tray or basket.

★ Rows of matching jars in glass or Perspex (I got mine at the supermarket) look fantastic on an open shelf with an assortment of items. Use to store dried foods, tea-lights, pegs, marbles, sweets or stationery.

★ Organize your cables under your desk or behind your TV cabinet using wire or food ties (for small wires) and plastic cable tidy. These days our home entertainment centres have so many wires they can look very messy if left dangling (and can be a temptation to children and pets, as well as create a tripping hazard). You can purchase cabling springs to gather the wires together.

★ Collapsible laundry baskets make great storage for soft toys.

★ Keep mops, brooms etc. off of the floor by attaching hooks to the inside of a cupboard – I have a couple of hooks attached to a short length of wood that is screwed to the wall in my utility room behind the door. You can't see it when you open the door and it keeps them out of the way of the cat dishes, which are kept underneath!

★ Do your pets have too many toys? As your cat and dog are unable to sort their own toys (I'm assuming!), take a careful look at this area of clutter too. If possible try to narrow it down to just one or two toys, but if you must keep more make sure they have their own tidy box to organize them away.

Feeling inspired? Stop right now before reading any further; go and organize something!

CHAPTER 6

Clutter in other areas of your life

*"Whatever results you're getting, be they rich or poor,
good or bad, positive or negative, always remember that
your outer world is simply a reflection of your inner world.
If things aren't going well in your outer life, it's because
things aren't going well in your inner life. It's that simple."*
— *T. HARV EKER*

It's a sure thing that if there is clutter in your outside life then there is clutter in the inside life too. We've looked already at how we reflect our innermost feelings onto the world around us. Clutter, as we've discovered, can be many things including a reflection of our anxieties, but often an anxious mind shows in our bodies too. I don't want to spend too long on this but it didn't seem right to write a book on the subject of house clutter without at least mentioning the mind clutter too.

Poor health

I know that things are going badly in my life when my body starts to – literally – fall apart. I have a skin condition called psoriasis and when I'm stressed my skin forms something called plaques. Raised areas of red and while scales form on the surface of my skin as it sheds in flakes. It's unpleasant and messy. When I am under pressure I eat badly and sleep badly – well, who doesn't? I also drink more alcohol than my normal one or two glasses a week. All these things contribute to making the condition worse. The chaos of my outside life literally becomes chaos on the inside and outside of my body!

Maybe when you have "clutter" in your working life (i.e. too many jobs on your plate that you don't want to complete or can't handle) you smoke more or eat more fatty or sugary foods to compensate? Many people do. In the end, everything about the state of your life and mind is tied together. Do you get spots when under stress? Maybe your hair goes dull or even falls out; sometimes hair can even go grey or white with shock or stress. Do you get a bloated stomach or regular indigestion? Whatever it is, your body will betray your inner turmoil.

But give yourself a break – we all do the best we can and I don't want you to blame yourself for your own coping strategies. I do, though, want you to notice what's happening so you can learn to cope a little bit better, see if you can eliminate some of this life clutter and get everything back under control.

What other things can be clutter?

Once you've got your house in order you'll probably want to have a close look at other areas of clutter in your life. The bottom line is that in every situation, something has to give – changes have to be made. You and everyone around you will get used to it, I promise.

Here are a few things that may be a problem for you.

Too many hobbies?

It's fun to join a sports club or join the local quiz night down the pub, but the problem starts when you also take on organizing the playgroup Christmas party; agree to do the sponsored run; help out at the local charity shop twice a week and attend an evening class … all at the same time. Take a serious look at your weekly activities and decide that you will limit them to one or two activities; this might include one club and one charity activity. It's possible to add in an extra every now and again but don't overwhelm yourself. You can of course change your activities after you've been doing one or two the same for a while, for variety. Make sure you have time booked in to do nothing at all. Sometimes the best activity is simply sitting in the sun, walking along the local riverbank, or spending some quality time with a friend or partner!

Taken on too much at work?

Perhaps you temporarily took over a colleague's work while they were away on holiday and now somehow the extra workload seems to have become part of your regular job? Maybe you were given a promotion without the pay rise to go with it; are they still waiting to see how you work out – twelve months later?

Another common problem is if a member of staff is made redundant or leaves and somehow the position is never replaced. Are you picking up all the slack and working later, starting earlier and covering at weekends to keep up with the extra workload? It's time to stop! Write down your queries (nicely! Get a friend to go over the points you want to discuss and keep a copy of the letter). Leave the letter with your immediate boss or human resources department (or both) and ask for a meeting to discuss the points. Take your copy with you. Discuss the points one at a time and have some solutions ready rather than just go for a moaning session!

Spending too long caring for others?

I'm not suggesting you give your children away, but maybe there is a way you can get a bit of a break once a week. Would a neighbour with children swap babysitting duties with you every other week? Can Grandma take the little darlings off your hands for a whole day once or twice a month?

We used to love it when our own children went to judo on a Tuesday night. My husband and I would rush off to a local pub (a different one each week) and have a bar meal! It was two hours of total bliss. Don't clutter up your children's lives with too many hobbies either. If they are already doing a sport after school and are members of the Scouts or Guides as well as an extra tutorial session then that's probably enough!

Do you take care of elderly relatives or a sick neighbour? I want you to see if you can share the burden of this a little. Now, you know this is going to cause trouble, but don't be made to feel guilty. You'll be a better carer if someone else takes a turn! Your doctor, healthcare worker or a relevant charity (a charity for older people, or in the field of the relevant illness) will be able to offer advice.

Too much studying

This might be a harder issue to deal with than many of the above. If you want to gain a particular qualification then obviously you need to put the work in; but there are some simple steps you can take to improve things.

- Take a break. Make sure you take regular time off from studying and do something completely different to give your brain a rest.
- Share study time with others so that it becomes a social event as well as a learning one.
- Find several different ways of learning to break things up a bit. Are your books available as an ebook? Your e-reader, like mine, may have a read-back-to-you button so you can listen to your study material as well as read it. You can even listen on the bus with headphones.
- Split the work into small sections and carry extracts in your car or handbag. Study while you're waiting your turn at the dentist or waiting in the car to collect your children.
- Give up one or more of your other activities for the duration of the study time. It's only mind clutter if there is too much going on.

No doubt you have other or different clutter zones in your life; perhaps going over the few above has helped you think about what some of yours might be.

Can you clutter-clear your life at the same time as clutter-clearing your home? How about clearing out your car, your handbag, or your desk or locker at work? The list goes on and on. Just remember it's an ongoing process – one step at a time, yes?

READER'S EXPERIENCE

I must admit I am minimalist – if there's anything I haven't used for six months then it's recycled or thrown out.

— *MARGARET*

Sit down with a pen and paper and make a list of the most stressful areas of your life and then come up with several solutions. Work through the list and tick things off when you have made the changes. Free your mind of clutter to keep yourself in better health overall.

CHAPTER 7

Watch and learn!

If it's not beautiful, useful or seriously sentimental,
remove it from your life.
— *ANTHEA TURNER*

CASE HISTORY
Clearing a bedroom

Background

A friend had just moved into a house with her teenage son and daughter and almost immediately her new boyfriend moved in. His marriage had broken down and his wife had left with the children, he was going through bankruptcy and was also an alcoholic and drug addict (my friend didn't know all of this at the time). *He* was clutter!

My friend's boyfriend was a very artistic person but also very handy. When he first moved in they seemed very happy; being out of work, he spent his days working on my friend's house, mending and fixing. It was a good situation for them both. After a few weeks he started to get bored of mending and began working on more creative craft projects round the house. Pretty though his panelling and carvings were, the main practical jobs (fixing the hole in the stairs, replacing the old, unsafe front door etc.) remained unfinished.

Months later the relationship went sour and eventually the boyfriend left (with some persuasion from the police). My friend was left in a low emotional state and jobs piled up around her. After much counselling she started to recover from this damaging relationship and eventually met and fell in love with a new partner. Immediately the work in the house resumed and progressed and her new partner helped out a lot, even though he already worked long hours. It was clear that the new relationship was stable and the energy in the house was much higher.

Yet progress on the house was slow because they both worked full time. There were still many boxes that hadn't been unpacked from when she had moved in twenty months earlier. This is where I came in. My friend needed motivating to remove rubbish and clutter out of the house and, at the same time, remove her ex-boyfriend's energy from the house.

Task

When I arrived at the house my friend's energy was fairly low, although she was very willing to follow my lead. We made a drink and then headed right for the bedroom with binbags in hand. The first thing I did was pull out everything from under the bed and pile it up on top. We started here. There were two plastic storage boxes under the bed already but they were too tall to slide under the bed easily; the bed was actually slightly "propped up" by them and to remove them we had to lift it up. I suggested we purchase new ones. I knew we'd be able to reuse the taller ones elsewhere.

Although I prefer that the underneath of beds to be kept clear wherever possible, in this case storage space was limited so I decided that four plastic storage boxes, lower than the existing ones, would work best and we measured the space we had available (always do this to ensure the best possible fit for the space). I also pulled out dirty clothes, shoes, an overflowing medicine box and a broken box of CDs that we sorted and organized too.

My friend had piles of boxes on top of her extended wardrobe so I asked her to lift everything down (we both got covered in dust in the process). I was delighted when she immediately began to vacuum the dust from the top of the wardrobe – her energy was increasing! The cardboard boxes were full of old clothes and other items not yet unpacked from her previous move. There was also a broken plastic box sealed with brown tape; I could see through the side that this had a box of weedkiller inside (not very good energy for a bedroom, you'll agree!). When we opened the box the smell was horrendous – it had also been packed with old dog biscuits and these had started to degrade. She was getting into the swing of things and the whole box, contents and all, went into the bin. Yippee!

There was also a large purple plastic box on top of the wardrobe, which we emptied and sorted. This box didn't go with the new pale-cream and pink colour scheme in the room, so as soon as we removed the box from the room the energy lifted once again. My friend wiped the lid of the box and vacuumed inside and it was repurposed for the garden shed.

In one cardboard box we discovered several items of precious gold jewellery that had become tangled up with all sorts of things including rubbish. She had no storage for the jewellery but had some free shelves in the bathroom. We measured the space available on each shelf and worked out what we could use to store the jewellery and some of the bottles and lotions she wanted to keep. She also had to take a lot of prescription pills and at my suggestion decided to store them in the bathroom cupboard too, which was safer than under the bed where they were currently kept!

I recommended we jump in the car (to give ourselves a break apart from anything else!) and drive to the store to pick up the under-bed storage we'd measured for earlier and the storage to go in the bathroom cabinet. I knew of various shops that would sell what she needed and we quickly picked up the new lidded boxes. Christmas wrapping and decorations were removed from various cardboard boxes and allocated space in their new home under the bed. If you're going to sleep on top of something be careful what you choose! Decorations are fairly harmless, as are bedlinen and out-of-season clothes. Paperwork or piles of books are not so good. If you have trouble sleeping, look at what you're "sleeping on".

My friend was not impressed with the plastic storage I'd originally picked out for the bathroom cabinet but selected some glass jars of various sizes. Of course I was delighted for her to select storage that she loved – I knew this way she would be more likely to use it! You have to love the storage or you simply won't use it. She was distracted by all the other lovely things on sale and wanted to look at other items, but I know from experience that speed is important – you have to keep up the momentum! This was where I could help; by keeping her on track.

We headed back to the house, had a cup of tea and a cereal bar for energy and continued working. When you start on a job like this you really need plenty of time as jobs can expand; just to finish the bedroom we'd had to do some work on the bathroom cabinet too. It was important for me that I didn't leave my friend in more of a muddle when I left than when I'd arrived.

She was very cooperative and really began to enjoy the whole process. It went very smoothly overall but the "stickiest" items spiritually were photographs and some inherited items; three watches and two pens that had belonged to her late father. She actually told me, "I don't use these, so don't know what I am doing with them but I can't part with them!" Once we'd cleared most of the clutter from the room we looked at them again.

We found a pretty box to put the photographs in. We've already seen that photographs can take several days to work through, but the important thing at this stage was just to leave the room clean, tidy and clutter-free. A photo-clutter-clearing session could wait. Then my friend was ready to make some decisions about the watches. She decided to give one away to another relative who came calling while we were clearing. I told her the rule: you hand over the item with love and then it's no longer yours. You give over the gift and the new owner can do what they wish with it (even if it's to throw it away!). She agreed.

I suggested she keep the other two watches with her jewellery so that she would see them and enjoy owning them on a regular basis (they weren't being respected where they were, dumped into the bottom of a cardboard box). After looking at the watches again she decided that she might even wear one of them – a great solution. The pens didn't work but they were good quality. I suggested she put both of them in her handbag so that she would buy refill inks when she next went to town and then she could keep one in her bag so she'd use it! She thought this was a great idea. The other was to be kept in the "gift drawer" we had allocated for all the wrapping paper, presents and birthday cards she'd collected (and stored everywhere!). She would be able to think of her dad every time she wrote out a birthday card using his pen. These solutions meant that she was really honouring her precious items.

My friend had two pretty hatboxes that matched her bedroom, but they were being kept in a place where they couldn't be seen, so we emptied them out and sorted the contents elsewhere. Then we placed them on top of the wardrobe to use for items that would rarely be used. Always put the things you use the most in the places that are easiest to retrieve and vice versa.

Conclusion

- My friend cleared several bags of rubbish from the room and several bags and boxes of items to take to charity. I always encourage people to take these items right into their cars if it's not possible to remove them soon. In this case there was a charity collection the following day so we simply placed them out to be collected.

- At first I was leading the clearout but as time went on I took more and more of a back seat and became designated dustbin-bag holder. Only occasionally did I have to ask, "Do you really want to keep this?" or "Why do you want to keep this?" (I didn't mind either way but I needed to be sure that the items she was keeping had real worth to her, or I wasn't being helpful!).

- As we removed things from the room, my friend became more and more energized; even at the end when I was flagging, she was still going strong! She worked faster and faster, spending less and less time mulling over each object: throw, charity, keep. We made little piles of "keep" items and after every couple of hours we'd stop and put them away, immediately finding a storage solution for them.

- She found money and precious items that had been lost.

- We removed decaying (dangerous to her health) items from the room.

- Photographs and some cosmetics still needed to be stored and sorted more efficiently but they were tidy when I left (old cosmetics and out-of-date medicines and creams were thrown away too).

- As I got ready to leave, my friend was walking around dusting and vacuuming her room – my work was done and the ex-boyfriend had been well and truly cleansed from the space!

It had taken us seven hours and a little expense (four under-bed storage boxes with lids, five large lidded storage jars and six small lidded jars) to complete the job.

Follow up

Once the clean-up in my friend's house had started, the rest of the place came together over the next few months. Clearing clutter energizes you once you get started, so why not have a go? Start with those small, easy-to-finish jobs or a small room like the bathroom.

Here is an example of a room-clear for you.

Clearing your bathroom

Your bathroom has the potential to be your sanctuary from the world. Imagine a spa-like room with candles, gorgeous bath products and clean fluffy towels. Imagine a beautiful mirror and one gorgeous plant, a lily maybe, or an orchid. Does this sound like your bathroom? No? Read on!

Is your bathroom full of children's toys and bottles of half-empty shampoo and conditioner? I sympathize. Mine used to look like this too. Clutter in the bathroom is something that most of us don't even notice in our own homes. If you ever have to use the bathroom at someone else's house, though, I bet you notice their clutter, right?

A bathroom never forgotten – for all the wrong reasons

I remember once going to a women's at-home sales party, a type of party-plan evening. I've long since forgotten what they were selling but I've never forgotten the bathroom. It was home to three small boys and I'm telling you, you could smell that bathroom from halfway up the stairs. Never – I repeat never – have carpet in your bathroom if you have tiny males in your household – they always miss the toilet!

Apart from the smell (which was the worst I've ever known), the sink and bath were filthy; every ledge and the windowsill were full of bottles, cans and children's toys. Even the floor was piled high with dirty laundry and toilet-roll tubes. There really was no hope! I was so shocked that I immediately went home and organized my own bathroom. I scrubbed and cleaned. Gathered all the spares (shampoo, bubble bath etc.) and put them in a cupboard. I left out one shampoo, one conditioner and one bath product (I put my own expensive bath-oil bottle into a sponge bag; I'm not daft – the kids could use the supermarket own brand!). A small selection of toys was gathered into a basket and we immediately went out and bought a bathroom cabinet.

The very next day I bought my daughters two bath towels each (giving each of them a colour) and a matching sponge bag. They had hooks in their rooms behind the door to store them and I trained them to take their stuff into the bathroom every day and take it back to store in their rooms afterwards. It really worked for us all as the best way to share our very small bathroom (and the only toilet in the house) between the four of us. Would something like this work for you?

READER'S EXPERIENCE

We have a really small bathroom in a 1930s house. What we have done is put shelves above the door to store cleaning products (so they're safe from children) and various toiletries. We also bought a corner shelving unit that holds all the shampoo, bubble bath etc.; it was cheap and designed especially for a bathroom. This year we hope to get a basin with a drawer unit underneath to store toilet paper and bath toys – I hate clutter!!

— *TRACY*

Many people favour special bathroom wire baskets to hang in your shower but I think that this can be a wrong step to clutter heaven. It doesn't take long for the shampoo to leave crusty drips on the wire and it's easy to stack up five bottles where one will do. If possible, find places to hide products out of sight. The bathroom in most houses is simply not big enough to have fifty products out on display. But why would you want to do this anyway?

Getting organized will also mean you can find things quickly and having the right type of storage for the job is worth a bit of planning.

You'll obviously need to keep your toilet cleaner and razors out of reach of children, for example. Even if you don't have children of your own, it's still better to keep things safe; most of us have visitors from time to time, after all.

Your plan of action

Remove as much of the "stuff" from the bathroom as you can and place the objects on top of a waterproof mat or shower curtain on the floor or a bed, ready to sort.

★ Carefully examine duplicates. Can you put all of the shampoos into one bottle? Only leave out one bottle of each product and store the rest away in a cupboard. Don't bring any new products into the bathroom until the old ones are used up.

★ Organize deodorants, hairsprays and so on in the same way. If you have a very small space, consider whether you could store and use items in another room instead – your bedroom?

★ Bar soap is really messy. Throw away grungy soaps and replace with new ones. Better yet, use hand soap, which is cleaner and easier to use. I have clear plastic pump bottles from the supermarket home section and use clear liquid soap; it's super hygienic-looking and very chic.

★ Matching items can help to bring a room together. You don't need to be obsessive about it but green toilet paper, towels (a different shade of the same colour for each family member) and shower gel can certainly help to create a coordinated and neat look.

★ If you don't have under-sink storage you'll have to be creative. Plastic organizers (the type you buy on a "coat hanger hook" to hang behind the door) can be really useful. Many DIY stores sell narrow sets of drawers or shelves created especially for bathrooms.

★ Buy a large bathroom cabinet with a mirror and keep your clutter inside and hidden away. We have a shelf but I still have the essentials in a basket – it really helps to create that spa-like feel in the room.

★ Make sure you have racks and rails fitted for towels and toilet rolls, for hygiene reasons if nothing else.

★ Did I already say no carpet? I did? OK – but I meant it!

★ Clean like your life depends on it. Pay special attention to around and inside the toilet. Do you have the right tools for the job? If not, get them! Rubber gloves are essential. Keep your cleaning products right in the bathroom if you can find a way of storing them safely, or have them handy in a nearby cupboard (your boiler cupboard might work as long as your boiler is lagged and it doesn't get too hot inside). Think safety first.

★ Try giving each member of the family their own (named or colour-coded) hook to hang towels and sponge bags on. This can be in the bathroom if you have space, or in bedrooms if not.

★ Remove any stray items from the bathroom back to the owner's room immediately! Make some new rules and stick to them.

★ Do your bathroom curtains need to go through the washing machine? Do you need a new blind or shower curtain? (Most shower curtains will go through the washing machine too.)

★ If you use bath mats inside the bath, don't bother to invest a lot of money in them. They easily get stained and spoiled by mould, so for safety's sake you're better off purchasing new ones regularly. If you're careful, bleach can work on newish stains, but once they've sunk down into the rubber there's not a lot you can do.

★ Likewise, use a cleaning product (I favour bleach here too) on an old toothbrush around your grouting. If it's still stained after you've cleaned off the grunge, invest in some grout paint to make the gaps between your tiles shine like new. By all means use earth-safe items if you have them; many of these are good and I'm not a bleach maniac, I promise! Use the products that fit your lifestyle and budget.

★ Dirty floor mats are a dead giveaway of a neglected bathroom. Buy mats with short fibres and wash regularly.

★ Trim pulled fibres from your mats and towels to keep them looking new.

★ Don't forget to clean your windows and once you're tidied and organized you might even have space for that scented candle or orchid you've been dreaming about. A pretty ornamented shelf on the wall at the end of the bath might just help make your dream come true!

Repeat around the rest of the house! Are you ready? I bet you are.

CHAPTER 8

Inspirations!

"Don't judge each day by the harvest you reap
but by the seeds that you plant."
— *ROBERT LOUIS STEVENSON*

Do you need a little help? Each house is different and this list might not work for your home exactly as I've listed it here, but it will give you a good place to start. Do you have your binbags ready, your cleaning cloths and your cleaning products? Grab some rubber gloves and an apron or put on some old clothes.

OK, let's go!

Front door/hallway

- Shoe storage: basket, cupboard, box. Only one pair of shoes per person should be kept by the door and only if you have the room
- Coats: hooks for visitors only (if you have a cupboard for family coats, try to keep to storing only one coat per person). Other family coats should ideally go into the wardrobe
- Key, wallet storage, letters: a drawer, basket or shelf works well here; find or buy something you like
- Clean the glass in the door and hallway, wash or vacuum floors
- Clean or add doormats, wash door curtains
- Remove everything else that does not belong in this area; throw, donate or return items to their proper homes
- Fabulous; now spoil yourself with an air-freshener for the entrance to your house (a plug-in type maybe or a gel freshener – whatever you like).

Lounge/sitting room

- Collect and throw away old newspapers, magazines and paper waste. In fact I would suggest you don't even keep a wastepaper basket in the living space. Remove rubbish immediately from the room instead
- Take out and wash any crockery that has made its way into the room
- Vacuum and clean floors, rugs and carpets
- Water plants or throw them away
- Organize book storage
- Wash or polish pictures, mirror, windows and photo frames
- Dust lampshades (check bulbs)
- Tidy away children's toys
- Straighten chair and sofa cushions
- Wipe clean coffee tables and TV stands and dust (carefully) electrical equipment
- Remove every item from shelves and mantelpiece, wash or polish shelves; only replace items you wish to display. Return everything else to its proper home
- To keep this room tidy do you need new storage? A magazine basket? A lidded box to keep hobbies in? A lidded box (just one!) for children's toys?
- To finish off you could add new scented candles, or air-fresheners or fabric-fresheners if you wish
- Well done! Now treat yourself to a new house plant.

Dining room

- Clear the table! Throw away paper rubbish and sort piles of clutter into boxes ready to be organized (in another room)
- Remove piles of non-dining-room objects from the room ready to be organized
- Remove tablecloths for washing, wipe table mats and table
- Wipe chairs (including chair legs) – do they need repainting or refurbishing?
- Clean pictures and mirrors
- If you store crockery and cutlery in this room, then you'll

want to empty the cupboard completely (if you are short of time, just work on one drawer or cupboard at a time)

- Throw away duplicates and items you don't use; place items for charity in a plastic box (remember to use a plastic box in a colour you don't like so there is no confusion over which is the giveaway box!)
- Vacuum or wash floor
- Take your "sorting" boxes into another room and work through them one at a time. Give yourself a deadline to complete the task (try doing this in front of the television – have a dustbin bag by your side)
- Dining rooms can be somewhere people tend to store things they don't use or want. Inherited things often find their way into this room. Remember, if you find it hard to throw something away, offer it to a family member (take a photograph and send it that very minute). If they don't want the item either, keep the photo and donate the item to a worthy cause or a collector!
- Congratulations. Now buy yourself a couple of new candles to add to the table. Eat by candlelight at the table tonight and enjoy all your good work.

Kitchen

- Kitchens can be a challenge. Any rooms you find too difficult to start are best broken down into separate smaller tasks (make a list of your own and tick them off one at a time; it really helps)
- The cutlery drawer: remove duplicates, throw rubbish, remove everything that doesn't belong in the drawer, wash and replace items you are keeping
- Cooking utensils storage: are your wooden spoons past their 'sell-by' date? Replace! Remove duplicates, wash and replace the rest
- Saucepans: check the safety on handles and lids
- Fridge
- Freezer

- Under-sink cupboard
- Look for crockery (especially mugs) with chips or cracks. For safety and hygiene's sake these need to be thrown (ever had a handle fall off a mug while you were holding a hot cup of tea? I have!). Look also for those sneaky "free" mugs (pottery mugs with horrible advertising slogans on). These are usually faded and stained, a double reason to throw away
- Are your tea-towels and hand towels still OK? Do you need to replace them? If not, sew on tabs so they can be hung up
- Wash down cupboard doors and inside every cupboard
- Clean sink, paying particular attention to the plughole, plug and taps
- Wash tiles, clean grout (you may want to use whitening here or re-grout if yours is messy)
- Sweep and wash floor
- Remove dead plants!
- If you keep paperwork in this room (first of all, why do you?) then make sure you have an efficient organizational and storage system. Open post and deal with it immediately to ensure a clutter-free space. Throw away advertising leaflets etc. immediately
- Set up an efficient recycling space
- Check out your cleaning products. Do you have too many? (Donate to a neighbour or friend.) Do you have loads of one product but not the thing you need the most? Remember, buying duplicates might be cheaper but if you only use one bottle a year you'll have to store the spare for a long time
- Note: don't mix cleaning products into one bottle in the way I suggested for shampoos. It might be dangerous.
- Clean your kitchen clock/timers. Check batteries
- Clean your hob
- Clean your cooker! (It's actually easier to give it a quick wipe each time you use it)
- Clean microwave
- Sort your "rubbish drawer" (everyone has at least one of

these). Contents may include pegs, rubber bands, carrier bags, bag ties, "useful" free things from crackers and the front of magazines, old lids, corks (why do we keep these?), lighters, paper clips etc.

- Take everything out of the room that doesn't belong here
- Feel smug and treat yourself to a bunch of flowers – display and enjoy.

Bathroom

- Wash bath, shower and sink (get those rubber gloves on and make sure you are using a suitable product to get rid of stains). I love products that remove watermarks and limescale and make your taps sparkle!
- Wash bathroom curtains or nets, wipe your blind
- Wash glass until it sparkles (windows, mirrors, shower doors)
- Wash floor (yes, get down on your hands and knees if you are able, or get someone else to do it for you)
- Ensure you have proper rails, shelves or a cupboard to organize your things
- Wash your towels
- Wipe sticky drips off bottles and jars
- Sort out the minimum you need in the bathroom and stick to this. Tidy away spares (maybe keep a list of the spares you have)
- Congratulations. Maybe now is the time to treat yourself to some new towels or a glamourous spa-like product?

Bedroom

- Strip your bed, turn and vacuum the mattress (get help here if you need it)
- Remove everything from the room (or as much as you can) and vacuum everywhere (move furniture around so you can get into the corners, but keep safe and use help)
- Wash windows, wash curtains if they need it, wipe out the windowsills

- Make your bed with fresh, clean linens (is it time to buy new?). Many people keep their old bed linens when they buy new – don't!
- Empty the contents of your bedside cupboards or tables onto a tablecloth or shower curtain (on the bed or floor). Sort, throw, clean
- Wardrobes, clothes drawers (these can take a while so maybe work through them another day (unless you are bursting with energy and raring to go!)
- Wipe clean all furniture (inside and out), check for broken door knobs, missing hooks etc. and replace
- Wipe clean bedside lamps, vacuum or wipe lampshades
- Take a serious look at ornaments in this space. Is it time to let some of them go? Alternatively find a glass-fronted cabinet to attach to the wall to save dusting
- Finished? Well done. Maybe you could treat yourself to a pretty bedroom throw, new lampshades or a whole new set of bedding?

Garage/garden shed/attic

- Usually a fairly large project. People shove everything in here! Gather together mass support. Have a skip, or volunteers with cars ready to remove unwanted items immediately. Bribe family and friends to help you by providing food!

A few tips

1. Useful storage includes plastic boxes with lids, available from many home stores and large supermarkets (sort and label boxes)
2. Attach shelves to the wall or use proper racking (reuse old kitchen storage items, look for unwanted storage being given away on Freecycle or request items in your local paper)
3. Use strong hooks to hang things up on the wall
4. Large items can have a designated "space" (label or mark out the space on the floor to keep the room tidy and so you can always find what you need)

5. Make sure boxes are rodent-safe (don't store food where it will get damaged/eaten)
6. Paint and poisons (weedkiller etc.) are part of most people's homes. Only store what you need and find a safe way to store it.
7. Bikes and other expensive equipment need to be secured
8. Use stacking storage for neatness – try labelling the shelves too
9. An old kitchen cupboard makes great storage for a shed/ garage
10. Only store items such as Christmas decorations and occasional holiday-use items (things like suitcases) in the attic. Most people have no idea what they have in their attics!

To be honest, if you manage to clear the shed, the garage and the attic I think you deserve a week's holiday somewhere to recover (or at least a nice meal out!). Well done, you've earned it. Sit back and feel smug and enjoy the lovely "light" feeling you now have at your beautifully organized and clutter-free home.

Still don't know where to start? Really? OK, let me remind you and inspire you one last time. Here are a few of those speedy "starter" jobs of various sizes to get you going.

• Check batteries in your fire alarms. Wipe fire alarms clean of grease and dirt
• Sort out your jewellery box
• Organize your sewing box
• Clutter-clear the inside of your car, wash and polish, vacuum (or just do the glovebox)
• Organize your music or movies
• Sort out your medicine box or cupboard
• Underwear drawer
• Handbag
• Clutter-clear your telephone address book (need a new one?)
• Cosmetic drawer/box
• House-plant hospital

- Wardrobe rescue
- Photographs (OK this is a big job but you will need to edit over and over so why not start today?)
- Bookcase
- Magazine rack
- Shoes
- Bedside drawer
- Sweep around your front door, remove weeds, add a plant of some sort, wash down (or even paint) your front door
- Gather up everything that needs mending, cleaning and sorting. I got shoes heeled, a bag seam stitched, jewellery stones re-glued into a ring and a gold necklace chain fixed. We also paid to have rugs cleaned, the leather sofa's faded patch resprayed and I sent back my expensive sunglasses to be mended. Many of these items were free or cheap to repair but getting them sorted made me feel fabulous.

Now let's have a look at the energy of a room and how it "feels". Sometimes if a room feels negative, that can be the whole reason it got cluttered in the first place.

Cleanse your clean space: modern feng shui and spiritual solutions

We've talked about how dirty and disorganized spaces can make you feel sluggish and lacking in energy. Likewise a clutter-free and organized space can help you to feel uplifted and energized.

There are things other than cleaning and mending that you can do to help lift the energy of the room once you've finished (or you could do it before you start!). Some are simple and others take a lot more effort. Have a look at the list below and select ones that appeal to you.

★ Paint the room. This isn't as crazy as it sounds. If you've recently moved into a new home and detest the colour scheme of clashing neon colours then it's going to be a lot harder to take ownership of the space. You'll also have to clear quite a bit of stuff (if not all of it) out of the room before you start painting. Before you know it you'll be halfway there with your clutter-clearing! See how this one works? The room will feel better in no time.

★ Wash down the walls. If they are just grubby rather than in need of repainting, a light rub down with a cream cleaner might do the trick.

★ Lift up and throw away the old carpet. Please note that if you decide to remove the carpet, you need to be prepared to replace it by doing something else – at least mopping the floor or, if more desperate measures are needed, sanding if it's wood, or painting it. This will take time and money, but there is nothing worse than beyond-repair, stained and smelly carpets.

★ Open the windows wide for a few hours. A blast of fresh air might be just what you and the room need.

★ Bring some fresh cut flowers into the space, or even better a live plant. Silk or dried flowers just don't have the same energy and, if they are dirty or dusty, can actually drag down the energy of the room.

★ Introduce an indoor water feature. This does take a little maintenance to stay at its best, so be prepared to put the effort in – it's worth it. It will want topping up with fresh water every day or so as it evaporates (or splashes) away and every few weeks it will want washing out with a gentle washing-up liquid (or an antibacterial spray if you leave it too long!). The moving water introduces negative ions into the room, which is beneficial for health.

★ Gift your room a "caretaker figurine". I have guardian-angel figures in every room of my house but you might prefer a religious symbol like a cross, or a goddess. I like to think they are watching over me and taking care of the room, protecting it.

★ I love to place crystals in my rooms too. Quartz crystal has a natural "pulse", which is why we use it in watches to help them keep regular time. Crystals can also do this for your home, keeping it feeling calm and relaxed. Why not give it a go?

★ I have various collections of tumbled stones (crystals with the rough edges smoothed off), placed in dishes in some rooms. In other rooms I keep individual natural lumps of crystal and some carved into shapes. Each crystal has its own energy; a specialist crystal book will give you more information about each type. I like clear quartz for my own home but why not visit a crystal shop and see what you are attracted to? Buy what you like and what feels right to you. Incidentally, you can also place crystals by your front and back doors to spiritually protect the boundaries of your home.

★ If you want to do a spiritual cleansing of the room once it's finished, why not smoke or smudge the room using an incense stick or smudging wand? It's really simple: buy a pack of natural incense sticks rather than a synthetic scent (I favour Nag Champa but choose whichever one feels best for you). Light the end of the stick and when the tip is red, blow it out. Waft the smoke around each room (you can use a feather to do this if you wish). Carry an ashtray or saucer to catch the ash as you go!

★ Alternatively you can follow the Native American tradition of smudging. This ancient technique uses bundles of dried "sacred" sage (white sage), sometimes mixed with other scented herbs like sweetgrass or lavender. Smudging is traditionally used to spiritually and psychically cleanse the room or space, removing negative energies. Psychic-mediums still use this technique today.

You'll need a small smudge wand (sometimes called a smudge stick); you can buy these from new-age shops and suppliers or on the internet. Gather together your wand, a lighter, a candle, some kind of ashtray, a large feather and a tray. Light the candle and then use it to light your smudge wand. You need a candle because the wand will often go out and it is easier to relight it with the candle. Blow out the flame and, as before, use the smoke to "cleanse" the room. You can simply move the wand around or use the feather to distribute the smoke more effectively. Take the smoke into every corner of the room. After you have completed the cleansing of your room, you can carry the whole tray to another space and start again.

★ Play uplifting music. Dance and sing in each room!

★ Light a candle and say a prayer or use a blessing of your own composition to sanctify each room when you have finished. If you prefer you can call upon the goddess or whatever deity you'd like to work with to bless your room. You might say something like this.

> *Beloved energy of our great Lord,*
> *please protect and bless this room and keep it safe,*
> *clear of clutter and a happy place.*
> *At all times I ask that the energy of the room*
> *be filled with your love.*
> *(AMEN/BLESSED BE/WITH GRATEFUL THANKS:*
> *WHATEVER YOU PREFER)*

CHAPTER 9

Questions and answers

"To solve any problem,
here are three questions to ask yourself:
first, what could I do? Second, what could I read?
And third, who could I ask?"
—— *JIM ROHN*

Q. What can we do about the stuff we have in self-storage?

A. "Our storage is costing £100 a month," one woman confessed. This couple were disabled too, so it really presented a challenge. People acquire and pay for storage but then have no idea what they have put there; yes I'm guilty of this one too.

Call in the help of a disability charity and see if they can help you to donate the items. NOTHING is going to be worth £100 a month! If you can't use it in your house now then it will probably never get used.

Q. I am a terrible hoarder. I've tried to make sense of why I am like this. I think it stems from insecurity and a fear of change. I would love to de-clutter and I have tried before but I always end up with a much larger "keep" pile than a "throw away" pile.

A. It's worth working alongside someone else – a friend with a binbag! Play fast music and work quickly. Have another box for charity items. When you decide to keep something ask yourself lots of questions: do I love this? When did I last use this? Am I likely to use it in the next year, two years? Or, if I like it so much why is it hidden away? Will I be displaying it somewhere or am I more likely to hide it away again?

We made a rule – NOTHING goes in the attic! Why is stuff in the attic anyway? If you want to keep it why aren't you using it now? Large suitcases and Christmas trees are the only exception to this rule.

Q. Help! I CANNOT throw away carrier bags, even though I only use a few of them as bin liners. What kind of weird fetish is this?

A. I am the same! To store carriers that you will use to line your small bins, keep a carrier-bag saver (a tube of fabric with holes each end, gathered together slightly with elastic). Only keep enough bags to fill it up. Make sure you always have a carrier tucked in your handbag and a bag of carriers in the car (you're more likely to recycle them). Many supermarkets even have carrier-bag recycling bins so you can recycle to your heart's content.

Q. My problem is I just can't throw anything out. I just have lots of clutter.

A. Start with one drawer! Empty all the contents, sort and throw; just make a small start and work from there. Most people fail to deal with clutter because they try to take it all on in one go and get discouraged.

Q. I need some anti-clutter angels; nothing earthly here is going to help!

A. Help is at hand! Ask one of your children to help; get them to ask you questions as to why you should keep something. It really works. After the clearing session, pay your young helper for their work. If you don't have a handy child, rent one from a relative or neighbour! ☺

Q. I really need to de-clutter; unfortunately I live with four men (my husband and teenage boys), who feel the need to keep everything. I also work full time, which doesn't help timewise.

A. One brilliant thing about clutter-clearing is that if you start to clear your own things, other people in your life will spontaneously start to "join in" by clearing their own stuff … strange but true! Start clearing your stuff and see what happens.

• • •

I hope you've found this book inspirational. I've loved sharing my tips with you. In fact reading and editing the book has inspired me to go and do some more clutter-clearing in my house! If you are a hoarder this is a life journey that is not easily solved in one or two sessions. Even I have to keep working away at the job. The biggest secret is just to start – choose a single drawer or box and give it a go. You'll be surprised at where that first step will take you.

If I look back over many years I can see I've come a long way. Many of the good habits have stuck – for example, I just don't bring new trinkets into the house any more. Make agreements with friends about the mutual exchange of gifts (consumables like flowers, scented candles, perfume and wine please!). This is a great way to prevent more items like unwanted Christmas or birthday gifts (which come with clutter guilt attached) coming into the home just to gather dust.

Don't forget the one-in-one-out rule for clothing and photo-frame pictures. Investigate your "sticky" areas or weird collections. Oh, and one final thing … I'm ashamed to say I still own that Chinese jug I bought as a child. Ah well, Rome wasn't built in a day!

I wish you luck!

Jacky x

Further reading and sources of help

FURTHER READING:
Clear Your Clutter with Feng Shui by Karen Kingston
DONATE:
http://www.uk.freecycle.org/
ONLINE CAR BOOT SALE:
http://www.bitsnbobs.co.uk/
CLASSIFIED SITE:
http://www.gumtree.com/
HANDMADE, VINTAGE AND ART SUPPLIES:
www.etsy.com/

Try your local council for collections of large pieces of furniture, pest removal etc. They can also help with local skip hire as well as your nearest recycling plant. Speak to your doctor about support for serious clutter-clearing addictions or ask to be referred to a specialist.

About the author

Jacky Newcomb is a multi-award winning, *Sunday Times* best-selling author known around the world as "The Angel Lady". Although Jacky is best known for her books of real-life stories of miracles and angel intervention, she has also published hundreds of articles about all manner of different subjects.

Jacky has been featured in many UK national newspapers including the *Daily Mirror*, *Daily Express* and *Daily Mail*. She's appeared on hundreds of radio shows all over the world and has been interviewed on national UK TV shows including *This Morning*, *Channel 5 Live with Gabby Logan* and *The Lorraine Kelly Show*.

After living with clutter herself and finally bringing things into some sort of order, Jacky has developed a special interest in clearing and organizing. This book is her personal story. Jacky is the first to admit she isn't perfect, and you don't need to be either!

Connect with Jacky online

WEBSITE:
http://www.JackyNewcomb.com
FACEBOOK:
http://facebook.com/pages/Jacky-Newcomb/117853386746
TWITTER:
http://twitter.com/JackyNewcomb

Other Jacky Newcomb titles

Heaven, Penguin
Call Me When You Get to Heaven, Little Brown/Piatkus
Angel Blessings, Octopus
Angel Secrets Collection Cards, Octopus
Angel Secrets, Octopus
Protected by Angels, Hay House
Healed by An Angel, Hay House
I Can See Angels, Hay House
Dear Angel Lady, Hay House
Angels Watching over Me, Hay House
Angel Kids, Hay House
A Faerie Treasury, Hay House
An Angel Held My Hand, Harper Collins
An Angel by My Side, Harper Collins
An Angel Saved My Life, Harper Collins
A Little Angel Love, Harper Collins
An Angel Treasury, Harper Collins

For more information about Jacky's latest books, CDs, DVDs, cards, personal appearances and other products and events, visit Jacky's website: *www.JackyNewcomb.com*

Modern Magic by Kirsten Riddle

Taking a wholly original approach to self-improvement, the innate magic within each person is harnessed in this spiritual survival guide that reveals how to utilize everyday routines and surroundings in becoming a better version of oneself. The book provides instructions on how to manifest what is needed to fulfill desires and needs, and for individuals to fully embrace the creative and contemporary aspects of themselves.

144 pages paperback · ISBN 978-1-84409-598-8

Soul Soothers by Cindy Griffith-Bennett

Featuring one-page meditations that can be practiced all day—while doing the dishes, waiting at the doctor's office, or even in the shower— this book is designed to calm those with busy lives. Whether for stress reduction or spiritual development, Soul Soothers brings peace to frenzied lives and provides the benefits of meditation without the burden of taking more time out of already overloaded schedules.

176 pages paperback · ISBN 978-1-84409-608-4

FINDHORN PRESS

Life-Changing Books

For a complete catalogue,
please contact:

Findhorn Press Ltd
117-121 High Street,
Forres IV36 1AB,
Scotland, UK

t +44 (0)1309 690582
f +44 (0)131 777 2711
e info@findhornpress.com

or consult our catalogue online
(with secure order facility) on
www.findhornpress.com

For information on the Findhorn Foundation:
www.findhorn.org